Dancing with God

Seeing God in the
Everydayness of Life

Roger Button

WESTBOW®
PRESS
A DIVISION OF THOMAS NELSON
& ZONDERVAN

Scripture quotations are from The Holy Bible, English Standard Version® (ESV®), copyright © 2001 by Crossway, a publishing ministry of Good News Publishers. Used by permission. All rights reserved.

WestBow Press books may be ordered through booksellers or by contacting:

WestBow Press
A Division of Thomas Nelson & Zondervan
1663 Liberty Drive
Bloomington, IN 47403
www.westbowpress.com
1 (866) 928-1240

ISBN:978-1-4908-3124-4 (sc)
ISBN: 978-1-4908-3125-1 (hc)
ISBN: 978-1-4908-3123-7 (e)

Library of Congress Control Number: 2014905467

Printed in the United States of America.

WestBow Press rev. date: 3/24/2014

I see from my house by the side of the road
By the side of the highway of life,
Those who press with the ardour of hope,
and others who faint with the strife.
But I turn not away from their smiles nor their tears—
Both parts of an infinite plan.
Let me live in a house by the side of the road
And be the friend I can.
Sam Walter Foss[1]

[1] Northumbria Community, *Celtic Daily Prayer,* (San Francisco: HarperCollins Publishing Company, 2002), 610.

Contents

Dedication

When I was in my final year of Seminary, I found a connection between Martin Luther, and Saint John of the Cross. I was given the opportunity to get my PHD in either Germany, where Martin Luther lived, or Spain, where Saint John of the Cross lived. Needles to say, I was excited at the opportunity. I came home and told Laurie (Laurie is my wife).

Laurie stood silently for a moment then looked lovingly into my eyes and said, "You are not dragging this family to Europe for six years while you are busy studying something only you and four other people in the entire world care about." She went on to say, "Your job is to put the cookies on the bottom shelf. Your job is to make Christ accessible to people."

After I got done pouting. I realized that Laurie was right. My job is to help people see Christ in the everydayness of their lives.

This book is dedicated to my wife Laurie. The woman whose job it is to keep me from getting to far into my own head and keep my feet on the ground. To the woman who has shown me unconditional love 99.9% of the time. I also want to dedicate this book to my dog Abe, a great friend and companion, a dog that has shown me unconditional love 100% of the time.

I love you Laurie, more than life itself.

Acknowledgements

Words cannot convey my deep appreciation to the people who have helped make this book possible. To the Clark County Family YMCA staff, who are busy everyday being Christ's hands and feet. They are a source of inspiration. To Corinn DeWaard, a great friend and a great person. Her thoughts and edits have made this book what it is. To Westbow Press for their dedication and Grace. They made this a joy to publish. Special thanks to Shaun Kauffman, your ideas and your ability to keep me on track has been invaluable. To Dr. Charles Conniry (Chuck), your friendship throughout the years has been a true blessing on my life. Your willingness to allow me to poke fun in the breads shows the true friend that you are. I cannot wait for the next ride. Thank you, each and every one of you. Know that you are loved.

Introduction

Dancing with God is a compilation of insights taken from my blog, *Daily Bread for Ragamuffins.*

I am a simple Quaker minister, more of a monk really. After spending time inside the walls of the church, I stepped out in front of the church in 2006. This is the story of how *Dancing with God* came to be.

In the little town where I was ministering, we had an ecumenical group. *Ecumenical* is a big word for a bunch of pastors from different denominations coming together to talk, to pray, and to encourage and empower one another. We would get together once a week. During one meeting, we complained that if everyone in town decided to attend services on any given Sunday, we would not have enough churches to hold everyone, but that our churches were nonetheless half-empty. (Yes, pastors complain too.) After this meeting, I told one of my pastor friends, "I am starting to have trouble with the 'Come and see' style of church where we ask people to come and give us a try. I am starting to feel led to 'Go and be.'"

I decided to move my office to a local coffee shop. This worked fine for a few months. I would find a spot at the coffee shop, and people would come and see me. It was a great arrangement. The shop loved it; people were buying lots of coffee as they sat and talked with me. I liked it a lot. I would set up shop and drink copious amounts of coffee while I talked with people. I thought everything was going great until one day a still small voice said, "I asked you to go and be, and you created another 'Come and see.'" That still small voice bothered me. It was right; I had created another "Come and see." I started to think, *What does it look, taste, and feel like to go and be?*

We had a YMCA in our little town. I called and asked, "Do you have any job openings?"

The person on the other end said, "Yes. We have weight room monitor."

I asked, "What is a weight room monitor?" The person described the job, and I said, "I would like to apply."

I met with the people at the YMCA, and they explained the requirements and told me the hours and the pay.

I said, "It sounds wonderful. I will take it."

They said, "Not so fast, cowboy. We need to see your résumé first."

I thought, *My résumé? It is a minimum-wage position and only four hours per week and they want my résumé?* I said, "Okay."

I went home and grabbed my résumé. Yes, I had one ready. I guess it is a pastor thing; we are always building our résumés. I brought my résumé to the YMCA and presented it to the interviewers.

They read it and said, "You would hate this position. You are vastly overqualified."

I responded, "I do not think that I would hate this position. In fact, I think it is right up my alley."

They said, "We don't think you understand. This job is mainly janitorial."

I said, "I read that in the job description."

They said, "No, really. You will be wiping down sweaty machines."

I said, "I figured that."

They said, "You do not have a problem with that?"

I responded, "If Jesus Christ can wash feet, I can wipe down sweaty machines."

They said, "Okay. We will give you a try."

On my first day as weight room monitor, I walked up to the cardio floor and saw a woman on a treadmill. She was running very hard; the treadmill sounded like a huge fan and was humming loudly. The woman was also crying very hard. She obviously was dealing with stuff.

She was working on her body, but her emotional and spiritual self was a mess. I looked around the room. There were many people in basically the same boat. People work on their outside selves but not on their inside selves.

As I wiped down machines, I started talking with these people. This YMCA had an indoor walking track, and people would ask me to make the circuit with them. They would tell me their troubles, and I would pray with them and for them. Before long, the YMCA asked me to be the facility's chaplain. I started writing what I called "Breads" after a staff member asked me, "Could you write an inspirational message?" The first "Bread" went out to six people within the Y, and in a short time the messages gained a national audience. I created a blog site so that more people could access them. I called it *Daily Bread for Ragamuffins.* The site quickly grew to reach an international audience and now has thousands of readers in many countries.

Dancing with God is a compilation of some of these "Breads." This book is meant to be ruminated on. It is my attempt to give readers a way to see God in the everydayness of their lives. I hope that through this book the broken will find healing, the hopeless will find hope, and most of all, readers will see that they are not alone.

As we drive down the road of life, we seldom get to see what God is up to as we look through the windshield. It is only when we glance in the rearview mirror that we get an idea of what He has been doing. The problem is, we cannot spend all of our time looking in the rearview mirror as we drive the car. If we did, we would run into a tree. We are forced to look through the windshield and trust that God is working in our lives. This trust is called faith.

Enjoy the book. Visit *Daily Bread for Ragamuffins* at http://rogerbutton.blogspot.com/ and let me know your thoughts.

Dancing with God

Good morning. I pray that the day finds you well.

The wind was blowing the other day, and I noticed a leaf being carried along. It blew one way, then another.

I watched as it went back and forth, tumbling over its stem, then over its tips. I sat for quite a while observing this leaf.

At first I was amused by the back-and-forth action, and thought about how the wind changed direction, causing the leaf to change with it.

I thought about how the leaf had no say in where it wanted to go. The wind was in control.

It occurred to me that most of us live and work at the whim of others. If someone decides to go in another direction or the economy takes a dip, our jobs might go away, and we will have about as much say in it as the leaf does with the wind.

Then God said, "Relax and watch the leaf."

I sat silently and did as He asked.

After a while, my heart began to change. I began to see the leaf differently.

I began to see it dance.

It no longer was an out-of-control leaf pushed here and there. The leaf was dancing.

A still small voice said, "This leaf makes Me smile. It is dancing with Me."

I watched the leaf for quite a while.

In the end, I was no longer thinking in a negative fashion. My thoughts turned to all the blessings and small miracles that happen every day. I just need to have eyes to see, ears to hear, and a heart to accept.

My prayer is that we all choose to see the beauty in God's creation, to see a leaf dance, and to ask, are we dancing with God or merely allowing ourselves to be blown out of control?

It is a matter of perspective.

Blessings,
Roger

People Tend to Make a
Lot out of Mondays

Good morning. I pray that the day finds you well.

It is the first Monday of the new year.

People tend to make a lot out of Mondays. They look at Monday as the start of a long week. They look at Monday as the end of a weekend. People tend to look at Mondays with a sense of dread. Fridays are quite different. People seem to get excited about them. Fridays carry a sense of urgency, like they must be completed quickly because good things will happen once they have been conquered.

Do you realize that workdays take up 71 percent of the week?

Do you realize that we will work for around the same percentage of our lives?

This makes me think.

If we spend 71 percent of the week with the sense of dread that Mondays seem to evoke, and if we spend about the same percentage of our lives working and carrying that same dread, aren't we wasting our lives?

It is the first Monday of the new year.

Maybe we should break with tradition and start looking at Monday with a sense of awe and wonder at what the week will bring.

Maybe we should be less concerned about what Monday will do for us and more concerned about what we can bring to Monday.

When I think about what God plans to show me today, my outlook on Monday changes.

I wonder what God wants to show you.

Something to think about.

Blessings,
Roger

I Woke Up Early This Morning

Good morning. I pray that the day finds you well.

I woke up early this morning.

Yesterday I noted that we tend to view Mondays with a sense of dread. But I said that when I think of what God plans to show me each day, my outlook on Monday changes.

I was contemplating this thought when I picked up one of my devotional books later in the day. This is what I read:

> Every new morning is a new beginning of our life. Every day is a completed whole. The present day should be the boundary of our care and striving (Matt. 6:34; James 4:14). It is long enough for us to find God or lose God, to keep the faith or fall into sin and shame. God created day and night so that we might not wander boundlessly, but already in the morning may see the goal of the evening before us. As the old sun rises new every day, so the eternal mercies of God are new every morning (Lam. 3:22–23). To grasp the old faithfulness of God anew every morning, to be able—in the middle of life—to begin a new life with God daily, that is the gift that God gives with every new morning ...
>
> Not fear of the day, not the burden of work that I have to do, but rather, the Lord wakens me. So says the servant of God: "Morning by morning he wakens—wakens my ear

to listen as those who are taught" (Isa. 50:4). God wants to open the heart before it opens itself to the world; before the ear hears the innumerable voices of the day, the early hours are the time to hear the voice of the Creator and Redeemer. God made the stillness of the early morning for himself. It ought to belong to God.[2]

Every day we have the opportunity to do good work, to empower those we lead. Every day we are given the chance to improve people's lives.

But it becomes very difficult to do good work when we are not at our best, when we are feeling that sense of dread.

Every day can become a teachable moment for us. Every day we are given a chance to teach. Every day we can give those we teach the opportunity to teach others.

The question then becomes, what are we teaching? Are we teaching the things of God or of man?

God wants to open the heart before it opens itself to the world; the early hours are the time to hear the voice of the Creator and Redeemer.

Are we taking time to listen for God's voice? When we take the time, are we truly listening? Have we opened our hearts or are they closed?

God made the stillness of the early morning for Himself. It ought to belong to God.

God made this day. Rejoice and be glad in it.

Something to think about.

Blessings,
Roger

---

2   Dietrich Bonhoeffer, *I Want to Live These Days with You: A Year of Daily Devotions* (Louisville: Westminster John Knox Press, 2005), January 4.

Spiritual Dry Rot

Good morning. I pray that the day finds you well.

I am still thinking about the Monday blahs.

We must meet every day as it comes, looking at it not just as a day in a week, or a year, or a life, or as one of many. As Dietrich Bonhoeffer put it, "Every new morning is a new beginning of our life. Every day is a completed whole."

If we looked at each new day as a blessing from God instead of as something to get through, our attitude toward life, ourselves, and others would be drastically different. If we saw each day as a blessing, the question would become, what do we do with this blessing?

Oswald Chambers has an idea: "Whenever you get a blessing from God, give it back to Him as a love-gift. Take time to meditate before God and offer the blessing back to Him in a deliberate act of worship."

He goes on to say, "If you hoard it for yourself, it will turn into spiritual dry rot."

Oswald talks about the danger of being in a hurry, the danger of the to-do list, the danger of an uncompromising schedule, the danger of special times for special things.

He warns, "Rushing in and out of worship is wrong every time—there is always plenty of time to worship God. Days set apart for quiet can be a trap, detracting from the need to have daily quiet time with God."

He takes this a step further and outlines what a holistic day, week, month, or year, or life would look like. He says, "There are not three levels of spiritual life—worship, waiting, and work. Yet some of us seem to jump like spiritual frogs from worship to waiting, and from waiting to work. God's idea is that the three should go together as one."[3]

Bonhoeffer and Chambers seem to be saying that we should take each day as it comes.

They seem to be saying that we shouldn't take ourselves too seriously.

They seem to be saying that we should allow God into the everydayness of our lives.

I wonder what this day with God will bring.

Something to think about.

Blessings,
Roger

---

[3] Oswald Chambers, *My Utmost for His Highest* (Uhrichsville: Barbour Publishing, 1935), January 6.

Hootin' and Hollerin' on the River

Good morning. I pray that the day finds you well.

One of the best things about our house on the river is that it's so peaceful. It is a place where a person can sit, relax, and learn how to breathe again. I like to say that it provides a "thin spot" to Christ.

Laurie and I have chairs that face the river, and we sit in them, listening to the water, reading, and watching for the deer that like to cross the river near our house.

The place is very peaceful unless our neighbor's nephew is having a party. Tuesday night as Laurie and I were getting ready for bed, the music started. It was country-western, and the speakers worked very well; the music was quite loud. When I left Wednesday morning for work, the music was still playing. Laurie told me that it finally ended around 9:00 a.m. Considering the length of time that the music played and the volume, which made it impossible to disregard, I will have to talk to this young buck about adding to the four or five CDs in his collection. I think I have most of the songs memorized.

Around 4:30 a.m., the thought did cross my mind to go over and tell the partiers to turn down the music and stop the hootin' and hollerin'.

I was not a happy camper.

Then my curiosity got the best of me and I wanted to see how long this party would continue. I found out.

Wednesday, Laurie and I watched as cars started to show up at the property. We decided to have a conversation with this group. We met the young buck's father, who was pretty embarrassed and said that it would not happen again. We left on good terms and went home.

I was pretty tired, and *The Bachelor* is not my type of television, so I went to bed early.

I awoke at 2:30 a.m. to more hootin' and hollerin'. I was ready to walk over and yell, "Shut up and turn off the music!"

I just finished reading *Walk in the Light and Twenty-Three Tales*, by Leo Tolstoy. One of the stories, "A Spark Neglected Burns the House," tells of two neighbors who come into conflict over an egg. The conflict becomes so big that eventually both their homes are burned to the ground.

We often talk about forgiveness, but it is hard to put into action. Tolstoy makes it clear that if the two neighbors had resolved the issue with the egg, both homes would have stood. Yet, reading the story, we see how easy it is to become myopic and narcissistic, taking a narrow view and thinking only of ourselves. Tolstoy makes this point about the neighbors.

As Christians, we are to put a better way into action. Laurie and I have forgiven our neighbor's nephew. We are a little tired, but not angry. We will have another conversation with him when the opportunity presents itself. However, we will do this out of love. A funny thing happens when you forgive someone you feel has done you wrong. You stop thinking about the situation and find humor in it.

Here is a story from another book.

Then Peter came up and said to him, "Lord, how often will my brother sin against me, and I forgive him? As many as seven times?" Jesus said to him, "I do not say to you seven times, but seventy-seven times.

"Therefore the kingdom of heaven may be compared to a king who wished to settle accounts with his servants. When he began to settle, one was brought to him who owed him ten thousand talents. And since he could not pay, his master ordered him to be sold, with his wife and children and all that he had, and payment to be made. So the servant fell on his knees, imploring him, 'Have patience with me, and I will pay you everything.' And out of pity for him, the master of that servant released him and forgave him the debt. But when that same servant went out, he found one of his fellow servants who owed him a hundred denarii, and seizing him, he began to choke him, saying, 'Pay what you owe.' So his fellow servant fell down and pleaded with him, 'Have patience with me, and I will pay you.' He refused and went and put him in prison until he should pay the debt. When his fellow servants saw what had taken place, they were greatly distressed, and they went and reported to their master all that had taken place. Then his master summoned him and said to him, 'You wicked servant! I forgave you all that debt because you pleaded with me. And should not you have had mercy on your fellow servant, as I had mercy on you?' And in anger his master delivered him to the jailers, until he should pay all his debt. So also my heavenly Father will do to every one of you, if you do not forgive your brother from your heart." (Matt. 18:21–35)

Love and forgiveness, two concepts we fail to totally understand.
Love and forgiveness, two concepts that we must continually work on.
Love and forgiveness, two concepts that we need to put into practice!

On a side note, would you please pray for me and my riding buddy? We are traveling the next two weeks. If you could pray that we have a safe journey and that we continue to see Christ in the everydayness of life and to feel His presence, I would appreciate it.

Blessings,
Roger

Welcome to the Poophouse

Good morning. I pray that the day finds you well.

I woke up this morning to the sound of crickets chirping. I thought, *How nice is that?*

After a few chirps, I realized it was my alarm clock going off. I mumbled some things, then turned it off and went back to sleep.

A few minutes later, crickets started chirping once more. I rolled over and turned off the alarm clock again.

I guess God wanted me to get up. As I lay in bed, I realized I had to go to the bathroom! This chore seems to gain importance as we get older.

I looked up to heaven and said, "Okay. I'm getting up."

So now I am sitting here in Mountain Home, Idaho, at a Kampgrounds of America camp, contemplating things.

When we got to the camp, my friend Chuck and I asked about Don, the guy who used to check us in. A new girl said he is retired and isn't doing very well. He has cancer.

We met Don a few years ago after a long ride from Yellowstone Park. It was a hot and windy day. We had been riding hard and were worn-out. Our bikes were out of gas, so this seemed to be a good stopping point for the day. We pulled into the camp looking road-worn. Don greeted us in his typical fashion. He is an old World War II veteran and a retired navy man. His speech and mannerisms come right out of old films. You know the ones I'm talking about. He is an old sea dog.

He has anchors tattooed on his forearms and the motto "Hold Fast" inscribed on his fingers.

I was in dire need of a shower, so I asked Don, "Are there showers here?"

He answered, "We got showers. They're in the poophouse." Now that wasn't quite what Don said, but I'm not an old sea dog. When he said this, I immediately pictured an outdoor privy with a hose attached.

I am not fond of outdoor privies.

"I will show you where it is," Don said.

He led us out of the main office and across the hall to a door with a code box on it. He typed in some numbers and opened the door.

We entered the most beautiful bathroom a camp ever had. It had marble floors, was very spacious, was air-conditioned, and had the best showers in the world.

"Welcome to the poophouse," Don said with a smile. I looked at him and he laughed.

Laurie and I live in a house by a river. We are closing on the house, a process that is taking longer than any of us expected. Laurie and I felt that we were in the middle of God's will regarding the house and could not figure out why we were encountering delays.

We were returning from our anniversary weekend. We celebrate anniversary weekends; this may sound over the top, but I know someone who celebrates birthday months, so we feel an anniversary weekend is just right. As we approached the front door, we found a package. We opened it and inside was a house blessing book. Caryn, whom we regard as one of the family now, gave us that book. We are buying the house from her.

I e-mailed Caryn to thank her; she e-mailed back.

Caryn is an amazing woman of God. She said that her family had started praying two years ago for just the right people to buy the house. We are no longer worried about the house. The closing will take place; everything will be all right.

Jeremiah 29:11 comes to mind. "For I know the plans I have for you, declares the Lord, plans to prosper you, not to harm you, plans to give you hope and a future."[4]

As Chuck and I rode yesterday, we thought about Don and about the poophouse. I also thought about the river house and Caryn.

When you relax and let God be God and trust in Jesus, it is amazing whom you meet.

Chuck and I will visit Don before we leave today. We will talk with him and pray with him. I'm sure Caryn and Laurie will be praying as well.

Will you pray for Don with us?

Blessings,
Roger

---

[4] Bible, *New International Version*, (Grand Rapids: Zondervan, 1984), Jer. 29:11.

Things a Horse Taught Me

Good morning. I pray that the day finds you well.

I realized this morning that I failed to tell you that Chuck and I ride annually. We spend the better part of two weeks roaming the country and seeing the sights. We started Sunday morning and rode to Mountain Home, Idaho. Monday we rode from Mountain Home to Fillmore, Utah.

Do you know what is in Fillmore? Not much.

Yesterday was a great day. We traveled through some pretty amazing country. As I rode along on my bike, I started thinking about Tinker.

Back on the farm, we had a horse named Tinker. She was half quarter horse and half Shetland pony. I guess that is why I have a dog that is half golden retriever and half basset hound. I seem to be drawn to the unusual.

Tinker was the horse that all the kids learned to ride on. She was a great kid horse.

Looking back, I was lucky to have been able to learn on Tinker. She had her quirks, though. She did not like saddles, so we all learned to ride bareback. Dad would put us on her back and she would start walking. At first, staying on her back was hard enough. I would quickly start to slide off to one side. Tinker would feel me sliding and would start walking almost sideways, twisting her back in a vain attempt to keep me from falling off. By the time I slid down one side or the other, she would be at a complete stop with her back twisted as far as possible toward whichever side I had fallen.

Then she would give me the classic Tinker look. I would be lying on my back on the ground, and she would crank her head around and look me straight in the eyes as if to say, "Moron, get up and get back on." I would do that, looking nothing like a cowboy in the movies throwing a leg over the horse and riding off into the sunset. A kid grabs anything he can hang on to, jumps the best he can, then scrambles and kicks his way back onto the horse. This was quite a process. Tinker would stand patiently, allowing me to pull her mane, kick her belly, and pull a leg over before finally sitting up on her back. She would wait for me to get ready, then start walking again. I would fall off, and the process would start all over again.

When we got the walking part down, Tinker would start trotting training. She must have had fifteen different trots. No matter how hard I kicked her or how many times I said, "Come on, Tinker; let's go," she would trot only a little faster. Trotting bareback is like sitting on top of a jackhammer. Have you ever seen a baby bouncing on a grandpa's knee? I am sure that is what I looked like. I was not very comfortable, but Tinker was a kid trainer. She would trot, I would fall off, she would give me the look, and I would scramble back on.

After I mastered the trot, Tinker moved on to cantering and finally galloping.

I was always amazed that we could be half a mile from the house and she would stand waiting for this goofy kid to get up and back on. The other horses would have bolted for the barn, free of their encumbrances.

Tinker finally taught me how to ride. By the time she got done with me, I could ride just about any horse. The horses would try to dislodge me, but I would sink myself into their withers like I had Krazy Glue on my butt.

As I rode through Utah, I thought about Tinker. I thought about how patient she was with me. I thought about how I might never have learned to ride if she had not taken the time to teach me, not just go through the motions.

As I rode through Utah, I also thought about the YMCA.

I thought how we have the opportunity to teach kids, adults, and families how to become whole. Psychiatrists would call it self-actuated. I thought what an awesome responsibility that is.

Tinker taught me how to be patient. She taught me that everyone is learning something.

I will try to do a better job of emulating Tinker.

I wonder how often Jesus felt like Tinker. He taught people, watching them fall and get back up. He never left them either.

I bet Jesus feels like Tinker with me sometimes. He never leaves me either.

Have a great day. I know that I will.

Blessings,
Roger

Honeybucket RV Rentals

Good morning. I pray that the day finds you well.

Chuck and I are in Flagstaff, Arizona. We have seen many wonderful sights and have experienced many wonderful things.

One thing that I have noticed is that there are a lot of RVs in this part of the country. We see many of them on the road and when we camp. Chuck and I like to stop at Kampgrounds of America sites. They have laundry facilities, showers, and bathrooms, amenities that become important the farther you get from home. We noticed many RVs in the campgrounds. Actually we noticed a lot of RV rentals. You can always recognize the rentals. They are clean and carry a big picture of something, better than a big picture of nothing, which I guess would amount to a white trailer wall. Maybe that is what the other RVs have—a big picture of nothing. We saw so many rentals that we started talking about getting into the RV rental business.

We noticed that many of the RV spots smelled really bad, in a sewage sort of way. We would watch an RV drive up and park. Then someone would emerge, drag out a big corrugated hose, and stick it in the ground. I bet you can figure out what the other end was connected to.

Chuck and I tried to think of a good name to call our RV rental company. Then after an especially bad waft of air, it came to me. I said, "Let's call it Honeybucket RV Rentals." But we realized that this name probably would not be a good marketing choice and decided not to go into the RV business. Thinking about it was giving me a headache.

In the morning, the RVs would leave, and we would watch and say, "There goes another Honeybucket RV."

I thought about that. All these people driving down the road had bathrooms complete with storage tanks. They had mobile honeybuckets.

I thought a little more and realized that our motorcycles do not allow us to take anything unnecessary. We are forced to carry the bare essentials. But we still have more than enough room to carry our own internal, personal garbage. In a metaphorical sense, we are our own mobile honeybuckets.

Then my thoughts turned to Christ and how He can cleanse us of all our personal garbage if we let Him. He can make us clean as a baby.

"Therefore, if anyone is in Christ, he is a new creation. The old has passed away; behold, the new has come." (2 Cor. 5:17).

I think I will let Christ do what He does best. Will you?

Blessings,
Roger

That's Why

Good morning. I pray that the day finds you well.

We are still in Flagstaff. We are going to see the Grand Canyon today. I have never seen it and I am pretty excited.

Last night in camp, a couple stopped by, and during our conversation they warned us about the thunderstorms that can happen here. They told us about the rain and the lightning. We had already ridden through a few of these storms. A storm in Nephi, Utah, was so bad we had to take shelter at a gas station. The lightning blew out transformers, and half the town lost electricity. Looking back, sitting in a gas station during an electrical storm was probably not the smartest idea.

My wife Laurie grew up in Minnesota, and I grew up in Kansas. Both places have amazing thunderstorms. We can talk about them all day, recalling how the thunderheads would come and the sky would grow dark and the lightning would dance across the sky.

Back on the farm, we had only one TV station, KLOE Goodland. It was not much of a station. The newscast resembled the one on *The Mary Tyler Moore Show* from the '70s. I think we had the original Ted Knight. There was not much on TV, so it was a good thing we had thunderstorms to watch.

Our house had a nice front porch with a swing. Unfortunately, my sister Katie and her friend Mary Ann, who lived on the farm down the road, once swung so hard that the eye bolts pulled right out of the ceiling, causing the porch swing to come down.

One day, Dad and I were sitting on the porch, watching a thunderstorm roll in; it was more fun than watching KLOE. Dad was sitting in his wooden chair, and I was sitting on the swing that was sitting on the porch. As the thunderstorm got closer and the lightning show revved up, Dad looked at me and said, "I wouldn't sit in that if I were you."

I looked at him in typical teen fashion and asked, "Why?"

The word barely left my mouth when lightning struck the ground in our front yard. The next thing I knew I was lying on my back, gasping for air, and wondering what had just happened to me. I was a bit scared, and I just lay there twitching. I must have shot ten feet from the porch swing.

I looked toward the porch, and I saw my dad approaching me. I started to prepare my response. He would say, "Are you okay? I was really scared when you flew through the air."

I would reply, "I'm okay. Thanks for asking."

Dad walked up to me, looked down into my eyes, and said, "That's why. Now get back up on the porch and sit in one of the wooden chairs before you get hit again."

I didn't ask why. I got up and sat in a wooden chair.

Many years later Laurie took me to the emergency room. We thought I might be having a heart attack. The hospital technicians hooked me up to electrodes. The results came back, and while I had not had a heart attack, I had suffered a reverse J, an event in which your heart stops at some point. My mother thinks it resulted from one of the particularly hard hits that I took playing ball. I know differently. I know that it stemmed from the day I asked, "Why?"

God is a lot like my dad. He will give you a nudge to do something or not to do something. Sometimes He will shock you right out of your boots if you don't follow His lead.

Sometimes He will look at you and say, "That's why."

I have learned not to ask why when God gives me nudges to do something or not to do something.

I have learned that I make a lot of mistakes but that if I do my best to sit in the middle of His will, as best as I can discern it, He won't have to use lightning to get the message through my thick head.

My dad loves me. I know that. God loves me. I know that too.

I have a reverse J as a reminder that I am not smarter than God or even my dad.

My takeaway from that experience is that when I hear the Spirit's soft, still voice urging me to do a certain thing, it is best not to ask why.

Blessings,
Roger

People Are Funny Creatures

Good morning. I pray that the day finds you well.

I am sitting on a bench at a Kampgrounds of America site in Big Timber, Montana.

We left home something like ten days ago. I'm not even sure what day it is now. I rode from Washougal, Washington, Chuck from Sherwood, Oregon, and we met up at The Dalles, Oregon.

We rode through Idaho.

We rode through Utah.

We rode through Arizona.

We rode through New Mexico.

We rode through Colorado.

We rode through Wyoming.

We rode into South Dakota.

We cut back again into Wyoming, and we are now in the middle of Montana.

We have seen some amazing things.

We have seen Bryce Canyon.

We have seen the Grand Staircase-Escalante National Monument.

We have seen the Grand Canyon's South Rim.

We sat in our chairs in Santa Fe, New Mexico, and watched the night sky. We saw meteors and watched as satellites raced across the sky.

We visited Mount Rushmore and watched a mountain goat steal the show as it entered the amphitheater. Tourists took their eyes off of Mount Rushmore and watched the goat do its thing.

I was amazed at all the people visiting the Grand Canyon. It was like going to Costco or Sam's Club or any other big-box store where throngs of people congregate.

We parked our bikes, and as we walked to the rim of the canyon, along with a gazillion other people, I looked over at Chuck and said, "I feel like a bunch of lemmings." When we got to the rim and saw people climbing over the rail to stand on the edge of the Grand Canyon, I was sure that we were lemmings. I was sure that at any moment we would all start jumping over the edge. Thankfully, no one went flying through the air.

People are funny creatures. They see one person do something and then they all start doing it. As I watched these people, my mother's voice was screaming in my head. When I was a kid, she would often say to me, "If your friends jumped into the Grand Canyon, would you?" These people's mothers must never have said that to them.

The Grand Canyon is huge. It is too big to comprehend. You cannot wrap your mind around the vastness of it. It is beautiful and grand. I guess that is why they call it the Grand Canyon. For me, it is a great representation of God—too big to wrap my head around, too beautiful to comprehend.

As I stood there, just looking, I thanked God for all the wonders that He has shown me, for the grace that He has extended me, for the love that He has displayed.

We live in an amazing place, but it does not compare to what He has in store for us.

In your everyday life, take a look around and see if you can spot the little miracles that Christ is doing.

Look for the wonders.

Look for grace.

Look for love.

Blessings,
Roger

Loving Others without Consuming Them

Good morning. I pray that the day finds you well.

I am in Missoula, Montana. Chuck and I arrived yesterday. We left Big Timber, had lunch at Mike's Burgers in Livingston, and arrived in Missoula around 3:00 p.m.

Before I left Big Timber, I gave my niece Hannah a call. She lives in Missoula. I had not seen her in a few years, and when she said that we should go to dinner after she had finished work, I was excited. I waited patiently for her to pick us up at the campgrounds at 7:30 p.m.

We went to dinner at Mackenzie River Pizza. It's a good place. If you are ever in Missoula, look them up. Tell them that Roger sent you and they will give you a pizza for twice the cost. Not really. They will look at you like you are nuts and say, "Who?"

We had a great time. We ordered Hannah's favorite pizza and some cheesy bread. I love to make Hannah laugh. She giggles when she laughs.

Hannah attends Montana State in Missoula and is majoring in sociology and gerontology. She has a real heart for the elderly and those in the sunset of their lives. One of the things that I love about Hannah is her heart. She has a very big one.

She discovered this passion quite by accident. While in high school, she took a job at a nursing home and found that there was a major need for help in this area. She learned that many people have no one and need a friend and a helper. Hannah decided that she would do what she could to make the lives of those she touched better.

Hannah is not in it for the money; she is in it because she cares.

Hannah is an upbeat, positive type of person who gives others hope.

Life has given her some bumps and bruises, but she doesn't let that get her down.

The last time I talked with her, she had a boyfriend, so I asked about him. They had split and her heart was broken, but Hannah kept the dog. She showed me pictures of this goofy, handsome pet, which looked very happy. Who wouldn't be happy with Hannah around?

As we laughed and talked and laughed some more, I thought about how Christ attracted people, how they flocked to Him.

Yes, He had amazing teachings. Yes, He was God incarnate. But He also was full of love—not the kind that feeds on others, but the kind that expects nothing in return.

Hannah has the love of Christ in her; she exudes it from her every pore.

If you cannot tell by now, I love my niece very much.

Hannah, I am very, very, very proud of you.

As I go through my day, I will try to be more like Hannah, since I believe that she models how Christ treats others, loving them without consuming them.

Hannah makes Christ smile.

I want to make Christ smile too.

Blessings,
Roger

Hospitality Is Not Hard

Good morning. I pray that the day finds you well.

I am in Richland, Washington, this morning. We got here last night. We pulled in to find that there was no place at the inn to lay our heads. The campgrounds were completely full.

Chuck and I left Missoula yesterday, but before we left we stopped by IHOP for breakfast. I am not sure why they call it IHOP; I certainly don't feel like hopping when I am done. As we ate breakfast, we started noticing things.

We noticed that the walls that made up the booths were very high.

We noticed that we had a feeling of isolation in this restaurant filled with people. We felt alone.

We talked about what it would look, taste, and feel like to bring a truly family atmosphere to a breakfast place. The atmosphere would encourage people to sit together, converse, and share their lives with one another. In this place, strangers could become friends.

We discussed what would make such a place.

First we would tear down the booth walls. In fact, we would remove the booths altogether. We would create a kitchen environment, kind of like a Benihana, where the chef would prepare a meal with all the people sitting around talking while he cooked, just as they would at home. Then we decided that the place should offer an all-you-can-eat breakfast so people would take their time, further enhancing the community feel.

Of course there would be plenty of pancakes and coffee at this all-you-can-eat restaurant.

We thought this was a great idea. We started thinking up names for our new restaurant. We thought the name should include the word *international*. It sounds impressive. We also thought the word *pancakes* should be in the name. The next part took some thought; we wanted to suggest a homey kitchen experience but convey something bigger, so we settled on *Ultimate Kitchen*. We also wanted breakfast to be more than breakfast. We wanted an experience.

We would call it the International Pancake Ultimate Kitchen Experience—IPUKE.

We were still full when we rolled into Richland last night to find that the Kampgrounds of America site was full. We were tired, we were hot, and we did not want to ride to another campground.

We just stood there.

We were reminded of ancient biblical times when travelers would enter a town and sit in the town square. They would wait for someone to come along and offer them a place to stay. They would wait for someone to show them hospitality.

Chuck and I were not invoking biblical tradition. We were just trying to figure out our next move when the innkeeper appeared. Actually he was the manager of the KOA camp. He looked at us and said, "We are all filled up, but you guys look tired. I do have one place if you don't mind camping there." (I thought he was going to pull a manger out of his hat.) He led us to a small patch of grass tucked in between a fence and an indoor pool and said, "It isn't much. How much room will you need?" We said that it would be perfect and pitched our tents.

Sometimes when you try too hard to create a space you get an IPUKE experience. Hospitality means looking at a person's need and doing your best to create a space—no matter how small, no matter how insignificant, no matter if it puts you out just a little bit—to make that person's life experience better.

Sometimes we come down hard on the innkeeper for giving Mary a stable to stay in. But he gave her a roof over her head, a place to lay her baby. In doing so, the innkeeper without knowing it gave hospitality to Christ.

How often do we miss our chance to be hospitable and in doing so miss a chance to be hospitable to Christ?

Christ said, "For I was hungry and you gave me food, I was thirsty and you gave me drink, I was a stranger and you welcomed me," (Matt. 25:35).

The righteous answered Him, "And when did we see you a stranger and welcome you, or naked and clothe you? (Matt. 25:38).

Listen to Christ's words. "And the King will answer them, 'Truly, I say to you, as you did it to one of the least of these my brothers, you did it to me.'" (Matt. 25:40).

I learned a lot from a KOA manager yesterday.

Hospitality is not hard.

Blessings,
Roger

God Runs the Show Completely

Good morning. I pray that the day finds you well.

I am home from the trip; I got back Saturday afternoon.

When I got to the house, I looked at my odometer and found that I had traveled 4,595 miles. I actually thought about riding two and a half miles past the house and back again just to make it 4,600, but my butt was sore and I was ready to get off the bike.

We saw many amazing things and covered a lot of miles. We had a great time.

Of course, there are things to be done post trip along with some honey-dos that always seem to accumulate while I am gone.

I unpacked my bike. I set up my tent, cleaned it, swept it out, repacked it, and put it away ready for next year.

I gave my bike a much-needed washing. It still had Arizona clay on it. I took it to a power wash rather than wash it in my front yard. I prefer taking my bike to a place that recycles the water. This way the soapy water is caught and reused instead of soaking into the ground along with all the other things that shouldn't be there. I think about things like this.

After I was done with the post-trip duties, I started on the honey-dos.

I changed the oil in three cars and washed two of them.

Actually, I found a place that was doing oil changes for fifteen dollars and took the cars there; they even threw in a car wash. I justified this by reasoning that I could not change the oil on my own for fifteen dollars, that I would not have to collect the used oil and try to avoid spilling it on the ground, and that I would be using a car wash that recycles its water.

I am an avid reader. If I am sitting somewhere, I will occupy my time by reading. There is nothing worse than sitting somewhere with nothing to read. In dire instances, I will read anything whether it is on walls, T-shirts, or hairspray bottles. It is amazing what is in hairspray.

Laurie and I were sitting in the oil changing place, and she had brought a couple of *Good Housekeeping* magazines. Someone had given her these magazines. The one I was reading was from May 2012.

I was skimming through it. Women's magazines baffle me. There is no rhyme or reason to them.

I ran across an article titled "She Inspires Me; Unforgettable Stories about Mothers and Daughters Who Found Beauty and Strength in Each Other." The article concerned two daughters who were the winner and the runner-up on *The Biggest Loser* television show in 2011. Sometime during the show, the girls came home for a visit. Betsy, the girls' mom, said, "Hannah sat my husband and me down for a candid discussion about what could happen to us if we didn't lose weight." Betsy admitted, "My size was weighing me down too. I was achy and lethargic, and I wanted that same feeling of freedom. I joined the YMCA."

Here I was, sitting in an oil changing place reading a women's magazine, when I saw another example of how the YMCA positively affects people's lives.

Hannah said, "My mom didn't have anyone to push her, yet she lost weight."

What we know but Hannah did not is that the YMCA is like family. We encourage, empower, and sometimes push people to keep going. We will motivate, give inspiration, and walk alongside people as they work toward their goals. We care.

I finished the article feeling good about the YMCA. I started flipping pages again.

After too many advertisements and mail-in coupons, I ran across another article, "My Faith Pulled Me Through," an inspirational story about a family and tragedy. A person quoted in the article said, "I think God runs the show. Completely. Life proves it every day: He runs the show."

I could not agree more.

After all, He is God and I am not.

Blessings,
Roger

I Do Not Want to Be
a Bathroom Door

Good morning. I pray that the day finds you well.

I was sitting by the river this morning, reminiscing about the ride. One of the things that came to mind was the question, what do you think about all day on a bike?

I do not carry a radio or anything that will distract me. I like to ride along just thinking about things. I never seem to get bored with my thoughts.

During our trip, we rode through the Navajo Nation, and my thoughts turned to the people living there. They feel that they are living in occupied territory. The consciousness of their hopeless situation is ever present. I thought about them a lot.

I also thought about bathrooms, in particular bathroom doors.

For the life of me, I cannot figure out why they open to the inside of the bathroom. I go to the bathroom only at a time of need; I do not go just to be there. I push the door open and enter. I do what I came to do, wash my hands, dry them, and turn to leave. This is when I notice the pull handle on the door. The handle is brass or stainless steel. Now I have a dilemma. There is no way of leaving the bathroom without touching the handle, which will make my hands germy again. If there is a paper towel, I can grab one and use that to open the door, but sometimes there is nothing but a hot air machine, which leaves few options. Opening the door requires imagination. Sometimes I have had to wait for someone to enter so that I could grab the door with my foot, kick the door open, and walk out. I have concluded that architects must have poor hygiene.

Many people walk into my office at the YMCA. They do not come just to be there but because they have a need. They will often sit and recount a hurtful experience. Many times they have gone to see someone about their problems and have left feeling germier than when they arrived.

I have a library in my office. Staff and YMCA members come in and grab books. I have a rule: there are no books in my library that I have not read. This way people can read a book and then we can discuss it together. One staff member is reading Philip Yancey's *What's So Amazing about Grace?* One story in the book concerns a woman who had had a rough life and made some bad choices and was contemplating suicide. A counselor asked her, "Have you tried going to church?"

Her response was, "Why would I go there? I feel bad enough already."

I think about that statement often.

When I talk with people, I sometimes have to correct them, and I try my very best to do this with love.

I do not want to be a bathroom door in someone's life.

I want a person to feel the cleansing power of Christ, not the germy sensation of judgment and self-righteousness.

Blessings,
Roger

One of My Morning Chores Was Feeding the Horses

Good morning. I pray that the day finds you well,

I am always amused by conversations. I like to track their direction. It is a fun pastime. Left uninterrupted, a conversation will typically end nowhere near where it started. I will often ask myself, *How did we get here?* A conversation is like taking a trip without a map or a purpose. You could drive along and at the end of the day ask yourself the same question. Sometimes the situation gets a little worse, and you wonder, *Where the heck are we?*

Many people walk into my office and want to talk. Sometimes I like to let conversations go just to see where they will end up. At other times I am laser focused.

Back on the farm, we had a dog named Fishmonger. She was a purebred Scottish terrier. I don't know why people give their purebred dogs goofy names. I guess that is why I like mutts. Nobody ever questions why you named your mutt Ralph or Larry or Abe. But a purebred is a different story; it seems that if you don't give it some outlandish name people will think you're weird.

Fishmonger was too long a name for everyday use, so we just called her Fish, which was even stranger. Eyebrows rose when we told people we had a dog named Fish. I think Fish would have been happier with a name like Cathy or Emma Jean. I suspect she was a little embarrassed by her name. When we called her, she pretended not to hear us. I bet if her name had been Cathy or Emma Jean she would have come lickety-split.

Fish was not just a good mouser, she was a great mouser; her favorite pastime was hunting mice.

My sister Katie had a cat named Bootslie. I am not sure why he was named Bootslie. I never saw him wear boots. For that matter, I never saw him wear shoes either. There was one time when I was sure he was walking around in Birkenstocks, but that is another story.

One day all of us kids were sitting on the living room floor, arguing. We were playing a board game, but Mary, the eldest and the boss of her smaller siblings, kept changing the rules, and the rest of us took offense. This always happened when we played board games. For the life of me, I do not know why we played them; I guess we liked to argue as much as to play the games.

We sat on the floor, Bootslie appeared with something in his mouth. I watched as he leaped into Katie's lap and promptly released a live mouse. Pandemonium ensued. My three sisters jumped onto the furniture, another tradition that baffles me, and started to scream. I was rolling on the floor in laughter; boys are not affected by mice the same way girls are. I don't know why.

Fish, who was lying next to us the whole time, sprang into action. She scooped up the mouse, ran to the door just as Mom opened it, then deposited the creature outside.

Bootslie never saw Fish grab the mouse and spent the rest of the night looking under every piece of furniture for her prize. I am convinced that Fish was a lot smarter than Bootslie, but don't tell my sister.

One of my chores was feeding the horses. Every morning I would take a bale of hay, break the leaves apart, and give each horse its share. (A leaf in this case is a section of the bale, not the foliage from a tree.)

Fish loved to help me feed the horses. She would wait by the bale, poised for the chase. I would let her get ready, then lift the bale quickly from the ground. There were usually three or four mice under the bale. When I lifted it, they would scatter in different directions. Fish would chase one, change her mind, then go after another. I do not think she ever caught a mouse when she helped me feed the horses.

Fish lacked focus.

Many times when I am counseling people, they want to throw me off, especially when we get to a place of pain or shadows in their lives. They try to change direction, hoping I will follow.

I am reminded of a conversation Jesus had with a Samaritan woman. As He talked with her, she kept changing the subject, but Jesus kept bringing her back to center. By the end of the conversation, she knew who He was, not because He told her, but because He did not let the discussion stray into left field. Read John 4:1–42.

Christ has taught me a lot of things. One of them is focus.

When we talk with people, let us have the focus to communicate Christ to them in a way that they will hear.

Blessings,
Roger

Our Ride Took Us through Albuquirky

Good morning. I pray that the day finds you well.

I am sitting here reminiscing about the ride. On day six, Chuck and I were wondering where to go next. We had visited Bryce Canyon, the Grand Canyon, and Sedona, all really cool places. Actually they were hot places, but they sure were neat.

We were sitting in our lounge chairs—yes, we take lounge chairs with us; they even have cup holders—and sipping our favorite new drink, Peace iced tea and lemonade. We discovered it on the trip. There is nothing more refreshing than Peace iced tea and lemonade after a long, hot ride. I wonder if I will get royalties for promoting this drink. I doubt it.

Suddenly Chuck said, "I have always wanted to see Mount Rushmore."

I said, "Mount Rushmore? That is in South Dakota!"

He said, "Thank you for pointing out the obvious." I took pride in that remark, since I have always considered myself the master of the obvious.

I said, "We will have a few days of long rides in front of us." Chuck just looked at me. Once again, I had proved my mastery.

The next morning we got up and took off, which was much better than taking off before we got up—although, I have met a few people on the road who I am sure have gotten it backward.

We decided to ride to Santa Fe, New Mexico. Our ride took us through Albuquirky. I know that Albuquirky is actually spelled Albuquerque, but Albuquirky is more fun to say.

Albuquirky is where I-40 and I-25 meet. We wanted to take I-25 north to Santa Fe.

Chuck took the lead as we rode. Someone pointed out that we looked like Mutt and Jeff. I ride a Sportster, the smallest of the Harley line; Chuck rides an Ultra Classic, the largest of the line. I could not help but think of a cartoon I watched as a kid. Mutt would follow Jeff, constantly asking, "Where we going now, Jeff? Where we going now?"

As we entered Albuquirky, I slipped into tourist mode. My head was on a swivel. I would observe the traffic and check my buffer zone, the distance between my bike and all the vehicles around me. Most bikers continually play the buffer zone game. I would take in the sights of the city, then return my attention to the traffic. As we neared I-25, we had to go left, merge right, then go left. I failed to see that Chuck had moved into another lane. I didn't notice until I was exiting the freeway and he was riding off into the distance.

I was in the wrong lane.

When I was a kid on the farm, I could not wait for Saturday morning at seven when KLOE TV broadcast *The Bugs Bunny-Road Runner Hour*. I would watch this show religiously, partly because it was so funny and partly because the alternative was to watch *The Hog and Feed Report*. Nothing against *The Hog and Feed Report*. I just did not find it particularly invigorating.

One of my favorite Bugs Bunny cartoons is the one in which he decides he needs a vacation. When Bugs goes on vacation, he does not take a bus, a train, or a plane. He digs a hole and pops up at his vacation spot. In this episode, Bugs wants to go to St. Louis, but when he pops out of the hole, he is in China and says the immortal line, "I should have taken a left at Albuquerque!"

When it comes to a letdown, nothing can match the sinking feeling of heading down an off ramp, watching your friend ride off into the distance.

As I rode down the ramp, Bugs Bunny came to mind. I should have taken a left; I hoped I wouldn't end up in China.

I went into country kid navigation mode. Country kids don't look for road signs; they look for landmarks. I rode the side streets, always keeping I-25 north in front of me. After about twenty minutes, I found an on ramp for I-25 north and took it.

As I entered the interstate system again and got up to speed, Tinker started to act funny. Yes, I named my bike after my horse. It was fitting. Tinker was white; my bike is white. Tinker was actually a pony; my bike can be classified as a pony. Tinker had a silvery head; my bike is chrome forward of the gas tank.

Tinker began to cough and spit, a sure sign that I was running on empty. I quickly changed my gas switch from normal to reserve—thank God for that switch—and continued on. I had about ten miles to find a gas station.

I was looking not only for a gas station but for Chuck. I sang, "I'm a cowboy. On a steel horse I ride," a line from an old Bon Jovi song.

Another reason I named my bike after my horse was that Tinker never left me stranded; she always got me home. My bike has been a great bike. It has never left me stranded either.

After a nervous few minutes, I spotted a Phillips 66 station, not my normal gas stop. I felt a nudge to go there. As I pulled into the station, my cell phone began to vibrate in my pocket. No, I did not download an app telling me when I am near a gas station, although that would be cool. Maybe I will develop a gas station app. On second thought, after the headache I got from the traveler's mug enterprise of 1972, I will leave it to Anthony, the app guru at the Y.

As my phone buzzed, I saw Chuck sitting in the gas station, calling me.

Chuck and I have ridden together a long time. I stopped at this gas station because I thought, *This is where Chuck would stop.* Chuck stopped there because he thought, *This is where Roger would stop.*

Once again, we were together.

Sometimes, during my walk with Christ, I have not paid attention and have found myself in the wrong lane. When I was young, it would take me much longer than it does now to meet up with Him again. But Christ has been walking with me for quite some time now. I still find myself in the wrong lane every so often, probably more frequently than I would like to admit, but we meet up much sooner now.

Walking with Christ was never meant to be easy, but it sure is comforting to know that while I may take my eyes off of Him, He never takes His eyes off of me.

I think Jesus got a kick out of me not paying attention and taking the wrong off ramp.

He taught me a great lesson that day.

Blessings,
Roger

My Zipper Broke

Good morning. I pray that the day finds you well.

Every year my friend Chuck and I take a motorcycle trip. We block out two weeks each summer to ride our bikes, seeing new places and places we have been before. We tend to have our phones off and to visit spots without reception. We do all this to force ourselves to detach, giving us the opportunity to decompress. We load our bikes with everything we will need to be out on the road for the duration: tents, sleeping bags, clothing. We take a lot of stuff.

The year takes a toll on us. Chuck has a high-pressure job, and my work drains me in terms of emotional availability. We look forward to this time away. It gives us a chance to heal, to contemplate life at a deeper level, and to return to our work presenting our best selves. These two weeks allow me to spend copious amounts of time with God. I spend much more time listening to Him than talking to Him. I always come back rested, at peace, and with a renewed sense of calling.

It is amazing what God shows me during my trips.

My zipper broke.

My saddle bag held many things that I thought I would need for this ride. The zipper broke as I was making my last predeparture check before leaving the house. This forced me to rearrange a few things. I came up with a temporary solution and was ready to go.

Chuck and his wife Dianne spent the night before the ride at our house, and the last thing we did together was pray over our trip.

I kissed Laurie good-bye, told her how much I loved her, and we were off.

At our first stop, I realized that I had forgotten a couple of things. The broken zipper had disrupted my preride routine, and I left some things at the house. Oh well, that's life. I did remember to bring my pocket Bible. It was in its usual place in my back pocket.

Chuck and I were pulling into a gas station in Sprague, Washington, when our ride took a turn that neither of us saw coming. As an old saying goes, life is what happens while you are busy planning for life.

My engine made a very bad sound. I called for a tow to the nearest Harley shop, which was in Spokane, Washington.

The driver showed up about an hour later. He was not in a good mood and did not look very happy. We got the bike loaded onto the truck, and I rode with him. Chuck followed us.

The driver's name was Brian. He noticed my Bible and said, "At least you have the Good Book with you."

I was not in a good place mentally. I just looked at him and smiled.

Brian started asking about Christ and God. He said he wanted to believe, but TV evangelists did not seem authentic to him. While the words they spoke sounded good, they seemed like salesmen. He said that he had tried to read the Bible a few times but never got through Genesis.

We talked during the entire ride.

I told him that I too had a problem with TV evangelists.

I suggested that he find a Bible that he could read, explaining that there were many translations. I said I was sure there was one he could understand. I suggested that he start by reading James, then go to John, Galatians, Matthew, Mark, and Luke in that order.

Brian asked about heaven. It seems that everybody ends up asking about heaven.

I said that all I knew was that heaven would be bigger and better than we could possibly imagine and that I was excited to find out.

He said, "I'm a good person, but I do not go to church. Will I get to heaven?"

I said, "You don't get to heaven by the number of times you go to church, and you do not get into heaven just by being a good person. In the Christian faith, we believe that you must accept Jesus as your Lord and Savior."

He did.

When we got to the Harley shop, Brian walked past Chuck and said with a smile, "This is all part of God's plan."

Smiling in turn, Chuck asked me, "What did you do?"

I said, "Brian and I had a nice conversation, and he is a new man."

The mechanics took one look at my bike and said I had a blown engine.

"Can it be fixed?" I asked.

They said it could but it would take two weeks and five thousand dollars.

This was a shock, not something that I expected.

Plans changed.

I was introduced to many new people. I met Paul, Sasha, Sandy, and eventually Beth.

Paul and Sasha were trying to get me to buy a new bike. Sandy wanted to see my credit.

I spent a couple of hours with Paul, Sasha, and Sandy.

My bike was done; there was no fixing it. I called Laurie and told her the news. She cried.

Beth is the owner of the Lone Wolf Harley Davidson dealership. It turned out that she was a good Christian lady. We had a great conversation, and she invited me and Chuck to eat dinner at the Harley shop even though it was closed party.

After dinner, Sandy gave me a ride with all my stuff to a KOA camp so I could sleep for the night.

The next morning, Chuck and I returned to the dealership. I was met with hugs, and my new friends told me how sorry they were for my loss. Paul said, "Roger, this really sucks."

I said, "Paul, while this is unfortunate, nobody got hurt; there are many worse things that are happening to people. I know. I work with them daily."

He said, "I know you do, and now I know how important this ride is to you and I feel terrible."

I replied, "Paul, it is not the challenge that defines you. It is your response to the challenge that defines you."

Paul looked at me and said, "I am going to remember that."

Beth asked, "What are you going to do?"

I said, "I am turning the bike over to you."

She replied, "Do you really want to do that?"

I said, "Beth, maybe you can get some money for it, and if it is in your heart, maybe you could donate the money to someone in need."

Beth looked at me for a moment, then said, "Roger, I will do that. We will be in touch."

Sandy said, "We will ship your stuff home for you."

Sasha was glad that I was going to wait and get a bike that I really wanted and not make an emotional buy.

I felt they cared about me and did not see me as a possible sale.

Chuck and I are paired up on his bike now.

God taught me many things that day.

I learned that if your eyes are open you can see His miracles even in the midst of your loss. Make no mistake. I was grieving the loss of something that I loved. But I knew that someone would be helped by the demise of my bike.

Who knows, maybe I would have gotten in a bad accident if this had not happened. Maybe not. I am not in charge of God's plans for me.

Through this incident, I was able to be a witness for Christ to a number of people. I also saw His compassion and care for me as I endured this setback.

My zipper broke

My bike died.

Brian has new life.

Beth called us disciples.

Paul, Sasha, and Sandy gave us blessings as we left.

If I could not see God in this, I would never be able to see Him at all.

Blessings,
Roger

I Have Been to Helena and Back

Good morning. I pray that the day finds you well.

I have been to Helena and back.

After my bike blew up, Chuck and I had some decisions to make. Since we were both on his bike, we had to scale back and ship all the items that we deemed unnecessary home. Lone Wolf Harley graciously agreed to do this for us. I was grateful, but we still faced questions.

Should we go home? Should we continue on? If we continued on, where would we go? Our trip was up in the air.

We decided to go to Missoula, Montana, stay the night, and figure out whether to continue beyond that. We considered riding down through Idaho to the southern end of the state, a trip we had made before, then heading home. This was a much shorter ride than we had originally planned, but a ride nonetheless.

We took off for Missoula.

When we arrived, we found a hotel, but it was booked up. We quickly discovered that there were no rooms available anywhere in town. In fact, we learned that there were no rooms available anywhere in the area for a hundred miles.

A marathon was taking place in Missoula, a big event that filled all the rooms even in the surrounding towns.

A "testicle festival" was being held in Butte, Montana, filling every room there and nearby towns. I am giving Butte the benefit of the doubt, thinking that the event had something to do with cattle and

46

the leavings of the neutering process that turns bulls into steers. I am hoping that's what it was. I do not know for sure. In any case, a testicle festival does not intrigue me, and for the life of me I do not know why it would be such a big draw that all Butte's hotel rooms would be filled up because of it. The event sounds a little off-putting.

We finally found a hotel room in Helena, Montana.

It was 6:40 p.m. when we left Missoula. I was still grieving the loss of my bike. I was emotionally drained. Chuck was tired. It had already been a full day.

On the ride to Helena, a pickup truck passed us and kicked up a rock, which broke the headlight on Chuck's bike. This was the cherry on the cake of our day.

Chuck was not happy.

There we were on the side of the highway. I was inspecting the broken headlight, and Chuck was doing an Indian dance and chanting.

I am not sure what he was chanting. I do not speak Indian. Chuck is not Native American, but I am assuming it was an Indian headlight dance he was doing. His face was really red at the time.

We rolled into Helena around 8:30 p.m. We were tired, frustrated, and pretty rung out.

When we checked in, we found out that the town was hosting a state championship softball tournament, a rodeo, and an antique auto show.

When I had called the hotel from Missoula, I had gotten the second-to-last room available in the whole town. Was our luck changing?

We put our stuff in our room and went to dinner at the hotel restaurant. We sat down and looked over the menu. Everything was fine at this point.

We both ordered the chicken fried steak with baked potato. The meal came with a choice of salad or soup. Our waitress suggested the taco soup, saying, "It is really good." We followed her advice.

Then Chuck asked an innocent question. "How about an appetizer?"

It had been a tough day, and evidently we were stress eating. I said, "Sure."

Chuck ordered jalapeño poppers, and I ordered chicken wings.

This was our mistake.

The meal began with a plate of hot bread and a huge bowl of celery and carrots. We ate the bread and the veggies.

Then came the poppers. We ate those.

Then came the wings. We ate them.

Then came the taco soup (complete with Frito chips). We ate that.

Then came the platters of chicken fried steak, baked potato, and corn. Not to be deterred, we dug into the main dish.

I got halfway through my plate when I hit the wall. My stomach looked like I was hiding a basketball. My temperature started to rise. I began to feel bad.

I was in Helena.

The cook came out to see us. He had never had anyone order that much food before, and he was concerned—and a little amused.

I returned to the room and lay down. I did not sleep well that night.

The next morning I felt much improved and was in a far better place.

Chuck looked at me and said, "We are halfway through Montana. Why not go to Duluth?"

I said, "Why not?"

Now we are on our way to Lake Superior, seeing country we have not seen, meeting people we never would have met. I get to see more of God's creation and spend more time listening to Him.

We never would have made this decision if we had found a room in Missoula.

We never would have made this decision if there had not been a marathon, a rodeo, and testicle festival going on. These things forced us to go farther than we had planned to put a roof over our heads for a night.

I am starting to decompress. I am starting to relax. I am starting to fill up again.

As I go through the road trip of life, I cannot see God's plan by looking through the windshield. It is only when I glance in the rearview mirror that I get a glimpse of what He is doing. But I cannot spend a lot of time looking in the mirror without risking running into a tree, so I am forced to look forward and to live in the mystery of His plan.

I am glad I have a rearview mirror. It gives me moments of perspective.

I am in Him and He is in me.

It is a good place to be.

Blessings,
Roger

Why Did You Put Him in the Chipper?

Good morning. I pray that the day finds you well.

"Why did you put him in the chipper?"

That's right: Chuck and I are in Fargo, North Dakota.

Did I mention that my wife is a travel agent? She has many beautiful and wonderful qualities. This trip has shown me another to add to that list. I simply tell her where we plan to be at the end of the day, and she has a hotel room waiting for us. This is much better than reaching a town and hoping for a place to rest our heads. This is much better than spending time searching for hotels during the day as we ride.

It's one thing I do not have to worry about.

We left Helena on Sunday. We rode on Highway 12, a beautiful Montana road. We saw plenty of old towns, pickup trucks, and cowboy hats.

Did you ever see the movie *Dumb and Dumber*?

As an old rider used to my own bike, I was feeling a bit like one of the two main characters in the scene where they are riding a minibike. I was experiencing this self-loathing when I saw something I had never seen in real life. We were just outside of Sulfur Springs, Montana, when we passed a minibike with two full-grown men on it. I could not believe my eyes. We stopped in Sulfur Springs for gas, and they pulled up shortly thereafter. These two young guys from Fremantle, Australia, were traveling around the country. They had been hitchhiking when someone gave them a minibike, which they were now riding.

I no longer felt so bad about being a passenger on an Ultra Classic.

We rolled into Miles City, Montana, that evening. This is a pleasant town out on the prairie. We arrived at the hotel that Laurie had reserved for us and settled in. Just outside the hotel was a pasture, complete with cattle.

Chuck grew up a city boy in San Diego, California.

I grew up a country kid in St. Francis, Kansas.

The cattle intrigued Chuck.

I said, "Just go up to the fence and call them."

Chuck looked at me and said, "Really?"

I said, "Really. All you have to do is say, 'Moo cow, moo cow, here cow, moo cow,' and they will come running."

I couldn't hold back a smile.

Chuck said, "You're making this up."

Recalling Tom Sawyer's words, I thought, *Huck knew I was joshing him.*

I admitted I was teasing Chuck but said, "You never know. It might work."

Never one to miss an opportunity, Chuck said, "I'll give it a try."

There is nothing funnier to a country kid than watching a city boy stand at a fence, calling, "Moo cow, moo cow, here cow, moo cow."

The cattle never came. One old cow did lift her head and gave Chuck a look before returning to her meal of grass.

The next morning we loaded our gear and headed to Fargo.

There is a lot to learn about being the passenger on a motorcycle. Just mounting the backseat took me awhile to master. Other things I learned as I went. One of them is to make sure that you are out of the way when the driver forgets you are there and clears a sinus.

I learned that one on the first try. Kind of like when I was a kid and my dad got me to pee on an electric fence. That happened more than forty years ago, and to this day I stay clear of electric fences.

North Dakota has a lot of interesting country and a lot of interesting people.

As I ride along, observing the passing scenery, I do a lot of thinking. I think about all the blessings that God has given me. I think about the work that He has called me to do.

Yes, life can and does throw curveballs at me, but I am reminded of a parable.

"Do not lay up for yourselves treasures on earth, where moth and rust destroy and where thieves break in and steal, but lay up for yourselves treasures in heaven, where neither moth nor rust destroys and where thieves do not break in and steal. For where your treasure is, there your heart will be also." (Matt. 6:19–21).

I think to myself, *Lord, today is a good day. I do not know what tomorrow will bring, but today is a good day.*

As I go through life, I know that I will have some pretty bad days. I know that some days will be horrific, almost unbearable.

I also know that God is with me every day. He will never leave me or forsake me.

That is one thing this country kid will never forget.

Blessings,
Roger

Okeydoke and You Betcha

Good morning. I pray that the day finds you well.

Okeydoke and you betcha. We made it to Duluth, Minnesota.

We left Fargo yesterday morning, and within five minutes we were in the middle of construction gridlock. As I sat looking at all the people headed in the same direction at the speed of nothing, I could not help but think about lemmings. Once every few years, these interesting creatures head out en masse and end up jumping off of a cliff. We looked like a bunch of lemmings—a massive sea of vehicles and people. I hoped there wasn't a cliff at the end of the road.

I often wonder about lemmings. Do the ones in the middle of the pack know there is a cliff coming up? Or are they just going with the flow with a great big surprise at the end?

I do not think there is a big difference between us and lemmings.

After a bit, traffic opened up. There wasn't a cliff after all. Before we knew it, we were in Minnesota.

You know you are in the North Woods when you see a wolverine on the side of the road. I bet you are asking yourself, *How many wolverines does it take to make Roger nervous?*

The answer is just one.

One wolverine is all it takes to make me think, *Hey, there is a wolverine on the side of the road, and my leg is hanging out for it to chomp on.*

We didn't have wolverines in Kansas, but we did have badgers.

A badger once made a nice little home near our house. I learned that it takes more than one cup of coffee for a badger to get rid of the morning grumps. It would come out of its hole when I walked by and do its waddle-run. (If you have seen a badger run, you know what I am talking about.) Of course, this would make me run, and I would yell over my shoulder, "Stop badgering me!"

I am convinced that is where the saying came from.

Wolverines and badgers. Don't mess with them.

I am sure we were quite a sight for the wolverine, Chuck in front, me in the back with my legs over my head. Chuck never saw the wolverine. Good thing. It is hard to drive a motorcycle with your legs over your head.

Minnesota is a beautiful state. We rode past towns like Baxter, Brainard, and Deer Lodge until we came over the top of a hill. All of a sudden, there was Lake Superior.

Chuck said, "It looks like the ocean."

I replied, "I told you so."

When Chuck mentioned that he had never been to the Great Lakes, I said, "It looks like the ocean."

Chuck said, "Really?"

I said, "Really. It does."

Somehow it felt good to say, "I told you so." It must have been my human nature coming out.

We checked into our room and went for a walk. We stopped by a YMCA and took a tour. It's a Y thing. We Y members tend to tour Ys when we see them. I guess it makes us feel more at home.

I told the people at this facility that I worked for the Y in Washington, and they said they needed to check to see if it was true. I wondered if a lot of people showed up and said, "Hey, I work for the Y. Let me in."

They checked on me and found out that I was a YMCA chaplain. They were curious as to how that worked. They had the typical concerns about inclusiveness and not being pigeonholed. We had a great conversation about not beating people over the head with the Bible and about how chaplaincy involves right relationships and being there for people in times of need. When I explained the meaning of chaplaincy, they wished their Y had a faith component.

The YMCA in Duluth is a great place, doing many great things.

After our tour, I could not help but think of my YMCA. I called my home Y to make sure everything was okay. When I left for the trip, an elderly member was in intensive care. A lifeguard saved her when she had a stroke in our pool. Her children were worried about their mother. We also have people with no place to live and people out of work. Our Y helps lots of folks.

Later Chuck and I took a stroll on the boardwalk. A woman approached and asked if I had any spare change. I reached into my pocket and gave her some. A person walking behind us asked, "Why did you give her money?"

I said, "I did for one what I wished I could do for all."

That baffled him.

Sometimes when Christ nudges me to do something, it doesn't make sense to people right away. Maybe this person will get it someday.

Or maybe he will be like a wolverine, trying to chomp on a leg when it presents itself.

I don't want to be a wolverine.

I know I don't want to be a lemming.

Lemmings and wolverines are wonderful creatures, but they're not for me.

Blessings,
Roger

The Best Stop Ever!

Good morning. I pray that the day finds you well.

"This is the best stop ever!"

That's what Chuck said after he found out that the Harley shop where we had stopped had everything he needed to fix his bike:

- a new headlight
- an Allen wrench that he could borrow to get the cover off of the motor and to adjust the ignition
- a bolt for his air-cleaner cover to replace the one he lost on the road

He has a vintage 1993 Harley with an S&S motor, so most places don't have these things.

We had ridden from Duluth to Mankato, Minnesota. It was a hot and humid day, and I was pretty rung out by the time we got to Mankato. Chuck had no idea just how good the stop would get.

After we fixed the bike, we rode over to Jim and Sandy's house. Jim is my wife's brother and is married to Sandy. I consider them my brother and sister, not my brother- and sister-in-law. Having an in-law would suggest that somewhere you have an out-law. I am not much into having an out-law, so why would I like having an in-law?

I have family: mother and father, brothers and sisters, sons and daughters, grandson and granddaughter.

When we got to the house, my father and mother were there. I will let you figure out the official relationship.

My dad, Jim, is an amazing guy. I will write about him one of these days. Today I am focusing on the best stop ever.

Sandy met us at the door and gave me a hug, even though I was sweaty and dirty from a long day's ride. Family will hug you even when you are sweaty and dirty. Dad and Bea were already settled in. I tried to help Sandy make up the guest bed. She was gracious, but I was in the way, so she asked me not to help.

We had a nice dinner, a meal that was more balanced than those Chuck and I have usually had on this ride. If you are wondering what I mean, read my post "I Have Been to Helena and Back."

Dad and Bea went home. Chuck and I got into the pool and stayed there until we were shriveled.

We ended the night with a great conversation, sitting on amazing leather couches that reclined with the push of a button.

This morning I am sitting in the backyard, looking at a 150-year-old cottonwood tree. Three squirrels are running around the tree, doing what squirrels do. Another squirrel is lying on the top of a fence with its legs on either side, head flat on the rail, tail lazily off to one side. I have never seen a squirrel that relaxed before. Pretty cool.

Sandy left for a meeting, and we ran out of coffee. She had made us a pot before she left. There we were, three men: Jim, Chuck, and I, staring at an empty coffee carafe. *We are grown men*, we thought. *We can figure this out.*

I hate to admit that it took three men to figure out how to make one pot of coffee. I made sure that the mess was cleaned up before Sandy got home.

When Sandy returned, she asked, "Who made the coffee?"

"We did," we said.

She said, "Okay. Who cleaned up the mess?"

We said, "We did."

How did she know we would make a mess? Women—men never will figure them out.

It really has been the best stop ever. I am completely decompressed and relaxed.

It is good to be with people who love you and care about you.

I will think about this stop for a long time.

Blessings,
Roger

Katie, Kim, Ruth, Mark, Beverly, and a Full Belly

Good morning. I pray that the day finds you well.

Chuck and I are in Rapid City, South Dakota.

I ran out of time yesterday morning, so I did not get the chance to talk with you.

The day before yesterday, we woke up to a wonderful breakfast and amazing coffee. Thank you, Sandy!

I went out to Jim and Sandy's backyard to relax for a bit, but my time outdoors did not turn out to be as soothing as I had hoped. As I sat contemplating their 150-year-old cottonwood tree, and very big, I wondered if there was a beehive somewhere in it or, worse yet, a hornet's nest.

Just as I was taking another sip from my coffee cup, a hornet the size of a hummingbird decided to say hello. I have found that the only way to get rid of a hornet is to do the go-away-hornet Indian dance. The hornet came right up to my nose, so I didn't waste any time. I jumped up, the coffee cup still in my hand, and started doing the dance.

I have never been a very good dancer, and this dance has many intricate moves and gyrations to it. I knocked over the chair, spilled my coffee, and finally gave up and ran into the house. I don't think I was doing the right dance. The hornet liked the dance and was dancing with me. I think I confused the go-away-hornet routine with the very dangerous come-hither-wonderful-hornet dance. The hornet continued to buzz around my head until I was in the house. Sandy asked, "Do you need more coffee?"

I replied, "No. There is a hornet out there."

She said, "Yes, we have hornets."

I said, "I know." Being a master of the obvious must be a family trait.

After a bit, we packed up to go. We met Dad at the Mankato YMCA and took a tour. It is an amazing YMCA. John Kind, the executive director, is a terrific guy, and these people are doing many wonderful things. I had a great conversation with Cheryl, the program director for social responsibility. We will talk more once I get home.

Our next stop was to see my sister and brother, Katie and Kim. They recently downsized to a nice home in Sioux Falls, South Dakota. Kim is Katie's husband and not my biological brother. Again, I prefer to avoid the in-law label.

We arrived just in time for me to go work at the mobile food pantry that Katie directs. I met many wonderful people who are having a hard time feeding their families. I met Mark and Beverly. I carried a box of groceries to their house and sat with them for a while. I prayed for them and gave them a blessing before returning to the pantry. There I met Ruth, an elderly lady taking care of her granddaughters.

Ruth is a hoot. I got into trouble shopping with her.

The pantry is arranged in a horseshoe configuration. All the food is set on a table and you walk through to get your share.

Ruth and I were holding up the line as we shopped. A pile of people were stacked up behind us as we debated the kinds of onions Ruth would like.

Katie finally came up and said, "Let's get a move on!"

I said, "Backer on down a minute, missy. Ruth and I are shopping."

"Backer on down" is an old Kansas expression. I guess "missy" is as well. I was proud of myself for combining the two old terms. Katie did not seem amused. I wonder why.

The pantry has cakes donated to it. They're wonderful! Katie said, "If a kid is having a birthday, give them a cake."

Well, I do not know how it happened, but every kid I helped that day was having a birthday!

I'm not saying that as we got to the pastry table I made up a story about a kid having a birthday. I would never do that.

By the end of the night I am not sure I was as much help as Katie thought I would be. That is what you get when you ask your brother to come see what you do.

I am very proud of Katie. She is the hands and the feet of Christ in her community.

Good job, sis!

Kim wanted to give me his Harley for the ride home and thought I could come get it later. It was a generous offer, but I did not take him up on it.

I love you, Kim! I hope this isn't too touchy-feely for you.

We left Sioux Falls around eleven yesterday morning. I called Katie from our first gas stop and found out that I had left my pocket Bible at the house. I will not see it again until I get home. I'm kind of bummed about that.

As we made our way to Rapid City, I reflected on Ruth, Katie, Kim, and Christ.

I thought about the apostle Paul, who tells us to take care of widows and children. I saw this in action at the food pantry.

It is always fun, and if I am honest, very humbling to watch Christ in action.

I will ruminate on "the hands and the feet of Christ" today.

Blessings,
Roger

Just Because I'm Paranoid Doesn't Mean They Aren't Out to Get Me

Good morning. I pray that the day finds you well.

I am writing from Buffalo, Wyoming. We arrived last night in this little town on the Western plains. It is a quiet place.

After checking in and putting our stuff in our room, we ate at a Subway. While the Subway girls were making our sandwiches, they started talking to us.

They talked about how there is nothing to do here.

They talked about how when they graduate from high school they will leave for someplace more fun.

I listened to their complaints. I listened to them dream.

I told them that someday they would grow to appreciate their home and how they grew up.

They looked at me and said, "How do you know?"

I simply replied, "Oh, I know."

Buffalo reminded me of my little town. There are times when I really miss it.

Getting to Buffalo was a bit of an adventure.

Chuck took his bike to the Rapid City Harley shop for an oil change and discovered that he also needed a new tire. It took about three hours to get everything done. A Harley employee gave us a ride to a truck stop so we could have breakfast.

At breakfast we met Charity. She was our server. She seated us in a booth and took our order. Then I noticed another booth that had an outlet. I was on my way to the restroom when I saw Charity. I asked if we could move so I could charge my iPad. She said, "No problem."

I asked if she could do me another favor. I said, "Can you go up to my friend and say, 'Move! Move now!'?"

We had a good laugh.

As Chuck and I sat eating breakfast, he told me he was sure that the Harley shop would charge him a mint. An employee had put a special sticker on his bike, and he was sure this meant the shop was going to get a lot of money out of him.

I said, "Sounds kind of paranoid to me."

Chuck replied, "Just because I'm paranoid doesn't mean they aren't out to get me."

I often wonder what this world would look like if we took the focus off of ourselves and put it on others. What if I could place all my focus on helping others, knowing all the time that others were focused on helping me? How cool would it be not to have to watch my back because everyone else was watching it for me, giving me the opportunity to watch everyone else's back?

It would be a fearless life, a life full of good, a life full of love.

I know this sounds crazy. I know it sounds undoable.

During the second Great Awakening, a little town in New York disbanded its police force. The town did not need it anymore.

As I rode through South Dakota, I ruminated on "the hands and the feet of Christ." I contemplated something Paul said to a group of people in Colossae, Greece. He told them:

If then you have been raised with Christ, seek the things that are above, where Christ is, seated at the right hand of God. Set your minds on things that are above, not on things that are on earth. For you have died, and your life is hidden with Christ in God. When Christ who is your life appears, then you also will appear with him in glory. Put to death therefore what is earthly in you: sexual immorality, impurity, passion, evil desire, and covetousness, which is idolatry. On account of these the wrath of God is coming. In these you too once walked, when you were living in them. But now you must put them all away: anger, wrath, malice, slander, and obscene talk from your mouth … and have put on the new self, which is being renewed in knowledge after the image of its creator. Here there is not Greek and Jew, circumcised and uncircumcised, barbarian, Scythian, slave, free; but Christ is all, and in all. (Col. 3:1–8, 10–11)

I often wonder what the world would be like if we followed this teaching.

Blessings,
Roger

A Flat Tire on the Road Trip of Life

Good morning. I pray that the day finds you well.

A friend contacted me, asking how I ended up being a pastor/chaplain.

I thought about her question and about what I like to call "the flat tire on the road trip of life."

As a chaplain, I get the opportunity to work with many people who have many hurts. Most of the time we can walk through their issues fairly quickly.

But there are those whose hurts run deeper.

Some have hurts that have completely stymied them. They are stuck and cannot make any progress because they cannot get past their pain. I have the chance to teach these people how to move forward, giving them the tools they need to overcome the hurt. I call this their flat tire.

When I was young I played football. I was good enough to win accolades and be offered scholarships to play in college. I had lots of friends and a girlfriend whom I was pretty fond of.

I went on to play football in college. I got hurt doing that.

One day I called my girlfriend to wish her a happy birthday. She said, "I don't love you. I never did love you. You were nothing more than a status symbol for me."

This did more than break my heart. I looked around and concluded that many of my friends were not friends at all. They were hangers-on, people who hung around because of what I could give them.

I felt alone, unworthy, unlovable. I could not shake this feeling. I was stuck.

I was experiencing a flat tire that I did not know how to fix. I stayed by the side of the road with my flat tire for some time. I was a mess.

It took time, but with the help of some very good and loving people, I healed.

One thing I have found is that if you let Him, God will use your hurts to help others.

I give people the tools to fix flat tires on the road trip of life so that the flat tires no longer define them but merely become footnotes in their lives.

It isn't fun being stuck on the side of the road, watching life pass you by, wondering if someone will stop and help you.

I know now that my girlfriend never meant to hurt me. She wanted to move on and did not have the words to tell me. She used the words she knew. I forgave her years ago and pray that life has been good to her and that Christ is the center of her life.

If you are having a flat-tire experience, find someone who will teach you how to change the tire so you can continue on your trip.

God means for you to live life to the fullest for His glory. He does not want you to stand by the side of the road as life goes by.

Blessings,
Roger

Hurt People Hurt People

Good morning. I pray that the day finds you well.

We spent the night before last in Buffalo, Wyoming. We spent last night in Rock Springs, Wyoming.

When we left Buffalo, we entered the Big Horn range. If you have never seen the Big Horn Mountains, you must add them to your bucket list. They are some of the most beautiful mountains I have ever seen.

Leaving the Big Horns, we entered Worland. There is nothing spectacular about this town, but it reminded me of someone I knew in college.

On my first day playing college football, the head coach sat all us freshmen down and said, "I have a wife and three daughters. If I don't produce, I'm gone. If you don't produce, you're gone. I will tell you when you are tired. I will tell you when you are sick. I will tell you when you are hurt. Don't worry about going to the bookstore to get your books. We have people doing that for you. Here is your class schedule and your football schedule."

My immediate thought was, *I should have had more fun in high school. This is a job.* I did not know at the time just how accurate that thought was.

I played half a season on a broken ankle. The trainers taped it up into a cast.

I dislocated my shoulder. They taped that up as well.

During one game, with three seconds left in the half, the other team threw a bomb. I intercepted it in the end zone. This presented a dilemma. I could run it back for a touchdown or kneel down and get a stat. I choose to run it back.

The field opened up before me. At the fifty-yard line, I saw a hole and ran into it flat out. Just then the other team's center filled the hole. We hit like two bighorn sheep. The kinetic energy was enormous. The impact did a lot of things that I did not notice at first. The crash sent me flying through the air with the greatest of ease. As this was happening, I kept my head up, still looking for the end zone. I landed on my feet, my body still going forward, and put my left hand on the ground to maintain my balance. Just as I did this, I got hit on the elbow, which was locked.

My elbow was dislocated. I went to the ground. I got a stat.

I started to notice other unforeseen consequences of the impact. Water-packed helmets had just come out, and I was wearing one. The force of the collision broke the water pack, and the hard plastic came down and broke my nose at the bridge. The combination of my head wound and the water made me look like I had ruptured an artery.

Blood was everywhere. The impact also broke the rivets on my shoulder pads and the tie string that secured the pads to my chest.

My parents were at the game and they thought I was dead. I looked like I was bleeding out, both shoulders appeared to be dislocated (they weren't), and my elbow was bent in the wrong direction.

I stood up, but I was a mess.

During halftime the equipment people and the trainers went to work on me like a NASCAR pit crew. The equipment people fixed my gear. The trainers fixed my nose and relocated my elbow. They taped me up, put an elbow brace on me, and pronounced me ready to go for the second half. The secondary coach told me, "Put your arms above your head." I did. One arm was touching my helmet because of the brace. The other arm was where it should have been.

The coach said, "Can you intercept a pass this way?" I said no. Then he ordered the trainers to remove the brace. You should have seen the look on my parents' faces when I started the second half.

Even this did not stop me from playing football.

A few games later, we were playing a team that had an all-American wide receiver. I was put one on one with him. By the end of the third quarter, he had no receptions and we were winning, 14–7. At the twelve-minute mark of the fourth quarter, I was speared. The player got up, saying, "I got him, coach! I got him!" He was kicked out of the game. I spent the next week in the hospital. The receiver went on to catch four touchdown passes in twelve minutes, and his team won the game. I guess strategically it was a good play for them.

That ended my career. The doctors told me if I took one more hit like that at best I would have one kidney, at worst I would be on dialysis the rest of my life.

My life changed.

Even after the doctors delivered this news, I was cleared to play for the next season.

My last game was the alumni game that spring. I had the opportunity to intercept a pass. Instead I simply took out the receiver. That is when I knew I was done.

That fall Oklahoma State called. The people there heard I wasn't playing, and they needed a free safety and wanted to know if I was interested. I cordially declined.

People were upset that I did not take them up on their offer. When Wyoming called, I relented to the pressure. I knew I couldn't play but went anyway.

This is where I met the girl from Worland. She was a great person. I was a butt.

She would ask, "Do you love me?" I would say no. I just could not go there. After a while she got tired of me. She got tired of being treated badly. She deserved better. She deserved the best, and that was not me.

After she broke up with me, she would watch me from a distance. I would catch glimpses of her standing there looking at me. She would have a sad expression on her face.

I was a mess. I hurt this person, and I am sorry for doing so.

Since my great healing, I think about her from time to time and pray, "Father, my prayer is that her life is better than she could ever have imagined, that she is happy and whole and strong."

I want to tell her that I am sorry. Perhaps I'll get the chance someday.

Hurt people hurt people.

Jesus heals people, and healed people heal people.

I pray my healing will continue to bring healing to others. I pray the same for you.

"Blessed be the God and Father of our Lord Jesus Christ, the Father of mercies and God of all comfort, who comforts us in all our affliction, so that we may be able to comfort those who are in any affliction, with the comfort with which we ourselves are comforted by God." (2 Cor. 1:3–4).

Blessings,
Roger

Another Day in the Old West

Good morning. I pray that the day finds you well.

Chuck and I are in Baker City, Oregon, almost home.

We left Burley, Idaho, yesterday. It was a beautiful run through some of the hottest weather we had experienced. Since we had decided to ride two up, we had to consolidate our things. This meant that I had to wear my leather jacket. There was no place to store it. The T-shirts that I had packed for the trip were all long-sleeved. If I keep the sun off of my arms, I won't feel poorly when we're done traveling for the day, so I have been riding in the backseat wearing a long-sleeved T-shirt and a leather jacket.

We rolled into Baker City, an old mining town (gold was king a hundred years ago), and checked into a hotel. Our rooms were not ready yet. We had forgotten that we gained an hour from Idaho to Oregon, and arrived an hour earlier than we anticipated.

I was rung out and vastly overheated. I needed water. The only place open was the lounge.

Chuck and I sauntered into the bar. Country music filled the air. I could make out a song about a girl dancing on top of a green tractor. I am glad we will be home soon. I miss my wife.

Chuck and I bellied up to the bar. (I am picking up on the country lingo in Baker City.)

Kate, the barkeep, said, "Howdy, boys. What will it be?"

In these situations, my sophistication shines. I screamed, "Water! Give me water."

My mind returned to the movie *Wild Hogs*.

Kate just looked at me.

I said, "Bring me water, and keep it coming!" Since I was in an Old West town, I added, "And bring a water for everyone in the bar— on me!"

There were only two other old greasers in the bar. They didn't even have the courtesy to say, "Thanks, long rider."

So much for Western hospitality.

Chuck and I sat sipping our water. We had already guzzled four glasses, prompting Kate to say, "Slow'r on down there, cowboy, or you're going to find trouble in this here town."

Suddenly the saloon girl (a waitress in an Old West town, as any western movie fan will tell you) approached Kate and said, "I have to go home. I can't take it anymore."

The girl looked distraught. Kate looked worried. They looked in my direction.

I summoned the saloon girl, pulled up one of the Breads on my iPhone, and asked her to read it.

She sat down, read it, then paused, staring forward.

After a minute, she asked, "Can we talk?"

I said, "Okay." Let's call her Jeannie.

We moved to a table and she sat down. Anyone who has sat down to talk with me knows what was about to happen.

Jeannie was a deeply troubled young girl. After listening to her story, I said, "Jeannie, usually I have more time to work with someone. Our time is short, so with your permission I will be a bit blunt."

Jeannie said, "Okay."

I went right to the heart of her flat-tire experience. She began to cry.

Over the next several minutes, I gave her tools to fix her flat tire.

Kate, a good friend to Jeannie, sat at a nearby table, not really trusting this water- guzzling cowboy.

After Jeannie left, Kate told me, "That was amazing. I have never seen anything like that before. Thank you for helping."

I told Kate, "I don't know how much help I was. I just tried to give her tools to help her cope."

God is funny. He doesn't care if you are on vacation or not.

A friend once said you cannot fire pastors; you can quit paying them, but you can't stop them from doing their job. I guess God knows that I feel retired. Since I am retired, every day is a vacation.

My prayer every day is that He puts people on my path so that I can give them a little glimpse of Him and His love for us.

God did not care that I was thirsty and tired.

I am reminded of something John tells us.

Now when Jesus learned that the Pharisees had heard that Jesus was making and baptizing more disciples than John (although Jesus himself did not baptize, but only his disciples), he left Judea and departed again for Galilee ... So he came to a town of Samaria called Sychar, near the field that Jacob had given to his son Joseph. Jacob's well was there; so Jesus, wearied as he was from his journey, was sitting beside the well. It was about the sixth hour.

A woman from Samaria came to draw water. Jesus said to her, "Give me a drink." (For his disciples had gone away into the city to buy food.) The Samaritan woman said to him, "How is it that you, a Jew, ask for a drink from me, a woman of Samaria?" (For Jews have no dealings with Samaritans.) Jesus answered her, "If you knew the gift of God, and who it is that is saying to you, 'Give me a drink,' you would have asked him, and he would have given you living water." The woman said to him, "Sir, you have nothing to draw water with, and the well is deep. Where do you get that living water? Are you greater than our father Jacob? He gave us the well and drank from it himself, as did his sons and his livestock." Jesus said to her, "Everyone who drinks of this water will be thirsty again, but whoever drinks of the water that I will give him will never be thirsty again. The water that I will give him will become in him a spring of water welling up to eternal life." The woman said to him, "Sir, give me this water, so that I will not be thirsty or have to come here to draw water." (John 4:1–3, 5–15)

Jesus is the great teacher and healer. He is God incarnate.

If I am to be the hands and the feet of Christ, I must be ready for any circumstance that comes my way.

Blessings,
Roger

Home Again

Good morning. I pray that the day finds you well.

I'm back at the river lodge.

I arrived home yesterday afternoon. Chuck dropped me off. We unloaded my gear from the bike and said our good-byes. He headed home, and I kissed my wife hello.

It is good to be home.

Chuck said, "It is good to get away, but great to come home. In the end we are both homebodies."

It was an amazing trip, filled with astounding things.

We had good days. We had bad days. We had great days. We had a terrible day. Our trip was a microcosm of life.

My bike blew up. This could have been a flat-tire experience. Instead God used it to bring a person to Christ. Someone else will be helped with the proceeds from the sale of my bike, and hopefully a group of people will look at life through a different lens. I will always have a soft spot in my heart for Lone Wolf Harley and the people there.

Thank you again, Paul, Sasha, Sandy, and especially Beth. Love you lots.

Riding two up on a bike taught me many things. I learned what it is to be a second seater.

We traveled through some of the most beautiful country we had ever seen.

We stayed in hotels. We stayed with family.

It was a pleasure to introduce Chuck to my family.

We saw a number of YMCAs. Our favorite was the Mankato Y, a special place.

I was able to see how my sister feeds those in need.

These were great days.

In Rapid City, Chuck needed a new tire. He had not expected this. It was a bad day.

Christ used the down time. As we waited for Chuck's tire to be replaced, He brought Charity into our lives. She now reads the Breads.

In Baker City, God brought me another very hurt person to talk with and to reveal a bit of Christ.

Laurie and I call the lodge our home. It sits on the bank of a river nestled in the Cascade Range. Just moments ago, two black-tail deer came out of the woods and crossed the river right in front of me.

At our old house, before we moved to Washington from Oregon, we had a pond in the yard that looked like a river. It was the brainchild of our middle son, Levi. We loved our pond. When we moved here, Chuck said, "You built a river at your old house and loved it. God gave you one of His to love."

I like that.

I am home now, and it feels great. I wonder what God has in store for me today.

May the Lord bless you and keep you. May His face shine upon you always.

Blessings,
Roger

Have You Ever Had a Nudge?

Good morning. I pray that the day finds you well.

Have you ever had a nudge?

I got home from Duluth a few days ago. When I tell people that I used my vacation to go to Duluth, they look at me kind of funny. I guess they look at me kind of funny anyway.

While I was on the ride, Sandy from Lone Wolf Harley e-mailed me and asked if I could send the title to my bike. One of the technicians is going to buy the bike as a project and put it back together. I was going to mail the title with a note and call it good.

Then I got a nudge.

As I sat looking at the river behind my house, a still small voice said, "Roger, I want you to call Lone Wolf Harley and check on them."

I do not make a habit of calling Harley dealerships. I definitely do not make a habit of calling Harley dealerships just to check on them.

I called. I talked with Sandy and said that I would send her the title. I thanked her once again for how the people at the dealership helped me during a time of need.

Sandy told me they had never seen anyone respond to a problem the way that I did. She said they talked about Chuck and me for days after we left. She said we changed the way they looked at things.

Then she said something I was not expecting to hear.

She said, "Can you talk to Sasha? One of her friends, an elderly gentleman, had a heart attack and is not expected to make it."

I said, "Absolutely." Sandy tried to find Sasha but could not. Sandy took my cell number and said she would give it to Sasha.

A few minutes later my phone rang. It was Sasha. She was in distress. She was not doing well and needed someone to listen.

I listened. As she spoke, I could hear sniffling. Sasha was crying.

She told me that her friend had come in to see her only a couple of days ago. They had a nice conversation. He left and she did not say, "I love you."

Sasha was chained to her regret. "If only I knew," she said.

After a bit, she became quiet. I asked her if she wanted to hear a story. She said yes.

Here is what I told Sasha.

I joined the navy in 1983. I was in navigator school down in Florida during the winter of that year. Coming from the high plains, I was not accustomed to eighty-plus-degree weather in November. To me, it was just plain hot. I never did get used to having my glasses fog over every time I walked outside. School was fun, but even though I had been to college, this was a very different environment and I missed my family. I would call home weekly just to hear my loved ones' voices and to find out what was going on. I usually did this on Saturday evenings. Those were the days before cell phones; pay phones were the only option. I could call collect or line up a bunch of quarters on the little metal shelf in the phone booth and be interrupted every two minutes or so by the operator, telling me to insert another two dollars.

I opted to call collect.

One Saturday evening I called home, and my grandfather answered. We called him Boppa. I do not know why. We called our other grandfather Grampa. I can never understand why we give things the names that we do. I try not to think about it. When I do think about it, I end up with a headache. I do not like headaches.

Boppa was a cool grampa. He taught me how to hunt. He taught me how to weld; he was a welder by trade.

Boppa gave the operator a hard time, claiming he had never heard of anyone named Roger. I yelled, "Just accept the call." He kept up the gag, and just when the operator was about to hang up, Boppa accepted the call.

Boppa was quite the character and always told wonderful stories. Nobody else was home, so we had a great conversation. As the conversation started to wind down, Boppa said that he was proud of me. I had an almost uncontrollable urge to tell him that I loved him, but I did not. We weren't that kind of a family. The guys would tell the girls that they loved them, and the girls would tell the guys that they loved them, but the guys didn't tell the guys that they loved each other. I could give a thousand conjectures why, but we just didn't.

Boppa and I hung up.

Two days later, I got a message from the Red Cross. The message simply read, "Your grandfather Boppa died. Call home."

I have been fairly lucky in life. I do not have a lot of regrets. The one big regret I do have is not telling Boppa that I loved him when I had the chance. I know that he knew I loved him; at least that is what I keep telling myself.

When I called home that day, my thinking had changed. Not only did I tell my mother and my sisters that I loved them, but I told my father too.

On Sunday afternoon we had a retirement party for a good friend of mine, Ken, and his wife Rachel. I was asked to emcee the event. As I talked, Boppa came to mind. I mentioned that so often we wait until it is too late to tell someone how much he or she means to us. How many times we let the moment pass without saying those words. I asked everyone not to let this moment pass without telling Ken and Rachel how much they were loved and appreciated.

Ken and Rachel know that I appreciate and love them very much.

My family members know that I appreciate and love them very much.

The other people in my life know that I appreciate and love them very much.

How important is it to let people know that they are loved? God tells us, "Better is open rebuke than hidden love" (Prov. 27:5).

It was the last lesson Boppa taught me.

After I told Sasha this story, she thanked me and was quiet for a moment. Then she said, "Roger, I love you."

I said, "I love you too, Sasha."

She thanked me for the call. She thanked me for listening. She is going through the grieving process. I told her she could call anytime and talk, yell, cry, or scream. I told her that I drew the line at hitting; you cannot hit a chaplain.

She laughed and said she would.

My prayer is that we do not miss any opportunities to let those we love know how much they mean to us.

Blessings,
Roger

The Cat's in the Cradle
and the Silver Spoon

Good morning. I pray that the day finds you well.

The cat's in the cradle and the silver spoon.

I was contemplating my bike the other day, and an old Harry Chapin song came to mind. As I sang the song in my head, the lyrics became:

> My bike died just the other day.
> It left the world in the usual way.
> A blown engine, too much to repair.
> They sold the bike while I was away.

As I hummed this to myself, I could not help but daydream of rides to come.

Then my mind returned to the original song. It is quite sad really.

The song is about a father who is terribly busy, consumed with the things that he thinks are important. They are trivial things, but all-consuming to someone who lives life worried about the future. The father never realizes that what is right in front of him is what is truly important. He recounts how the little boy would say, "When I grow up, I want to be just like you." The pride in the father's voice is clear when he sings this. Then the little boy grows up, and the father discovers that his son has turned out to be just like him, too busy for his father. The father is left all alone, wanting the only thing that he cannot have, time with his son.

As I pondered this, another visual came to mind. It was from the movie *Hook*. In the scene, Robin Williams, who plays a father consumed with climbing the ladder and making money, is standing at a window. His wife has put the children to bed. She walks in and says, "Peter, you are not paying attention. Your children are growing up and you are missing it."

> My bike died the just other day.
> It left the world in the usual way.
> A blown engine, too much to repair.
> They sold the bike while I was away.

Brother Lawrence was a Carmelite monk in the 1600s. He was not well schooled, and became a monk at an older age than most. The other monks thought him not up to the task of "high spirituality." He was relegated to kitchen duty. He would shop for food, prepare it, and clean up after the meals. He did this so that the other monks would not be distracted from their devotions.

As Brother Lawrence went through his day, he focused on the presence of God. When he went to the market, he would buy food as if he were going to feed God. When he prepared a meal, it was a meal for God. When he washed the dishes, he washed dishes for God.

The funny thing is, we do not study the other monks. We study Brother Lawrence. We study his book, *The Practice of the Presence of God*. The other monks, who spent their time in the sanctuary, we do not know. Brother Lawrence, who spent much less time in the sanctuary and much more time serving, we do know.

It is good to contemplate the things of God. It is good to daydream of heaven and being in relationship with Him. Christ never meant for us to be so focused on Him that we let the world and those around us go to hell.

I know that Christ is focused on me; He is not standing with His back to me, looking out of a window and contemplating the future. He is not so consumed with the future that He says, "Not now," when I want to talk with Him.

Let us use Christ's example to shape our lives.

Lord, don't let me become the father in "Cat's in the Cradle." Please remind me when I am not being present to the people You want me to be present to. Teach me to be Brother Lawrence. Put people in front of me, Lord, so that they may get a glimpse of You, as I am in You and You are in me. Amen.

Blessings,
Roger

I've Got Nothing

Good morning. I pray that the day finds you well.

Have you ever had one of those days when you've got nothing?

It's not a particularly bad day. It's not a particularly good day.

I would call it a normal day.

I got up this morning and had my quiet time. No big revelations there.

I took a shower, the water cascading over my head, waiting for something.

Nothing.

I drove to the YMCA, waiting.

Nothing.

I took my aqua aerobics class.

Nothing.

I talk a lot about living in the mystery.

Living in the mystery means taking each day as it comes. Instead of trying to figure out what God is up to, you wait for Him to show you what He wants you to do.

Often this means waiting. You wait for Him to direct your actions.

I am not saying that you should do nothing. I am not saying that at all.

You must still live your life. You must still go through the day being Christ's hands and feet.

What I am saying is, don't push God to give you something special to do or to say. He will do this in His perfect timing.

It's okay to say, "I've got nothing."

It's okay to wait.

Lord, I wait. I wait for You. I am doing my best to do Your will, not my will. Help me to do Your will. In the words of Isaiah, "Here am I, Lord. Send me." Father, I am only human. It is hard to wait, but I am waiting. Forgive my impatience; forgive my nagging. It is hard to wait. I love You, Lord. Amen.

Blessings,
Roger

This old house

Good morning,

I pray that the day finds you well.

I awoke extra late this morning, I slept hard. The house that Laurie and I live in is conducive to relaxing, contemplating, and sleeping. It is an old house that someone loved for a lifetime, grew old, eventually left the house to live in an assisted community and eventually died. The house has sat vacant for a number of years. There was no one to live in it and it too started to feel its age. It is in the country, next to a river, and does not have the noise that one typically associates with living in town; it is not silent though. There is the sound of the river that flows past our house, there is the sound of the breeze that rustles the leaves in the trees, there are the sounds of the birds talking. Ducks can be seen swimming along the river's banks. There are even the sounds of something living in our walls. The first time I looked at the house I thought, "nice location but it needs a lot of TLC." Laurie saw the house and thought, "This is home." As we discussed the house, I would tell her all the things wrong with the house, and she would tell me, "Look at all the possibilities." During our "house hunting" experience we looked at over 60 homes. During our house hunting experience we kept coming back to this house. To be honest, at first I was just placating Laurie. I would agree to come look at the river house because it made her happy to look at it. Over time, I started to catch her vision for the house. Over time, I too began to see "all the possibilities." I could see the houses potential.

This morning, I am sitting in the house talking with you. As I contemplate this house, I am thinking about Christ, I am thinking about Satan. Satan, would be the one who would look at me and tell Christ, "Look at that old guy. He is broken, he is a mess. He is not worth the time it would take to fix him up and make him whole and strong and healthy." Christ would say, "Look at all the possibilities." As I think about this, I realize that I had the mindset of Satan regarding this house; Laurie had the mindset of Christ. Satan likes to look at all the negative things in the world and point them out. Christ, while never being blind to the things that are broken still has the ability to see the potential, the possibilities, the goodness that people have in them, no matter how hidden this goodness is. Satan likes to create noise. Christ likes to create tranquility. I am so glad the Christ was not afraid of the things that were living in my walls. I am so glad the He took the time to work on my house. I am so glad that He looks at my house as a project, a work in progress. I am so glad that Christ loves me and wants to live in me. Christ loves you too. Christ likes to live in you. Satan likes to keep things vacant, alone, unloved and dilapidated. What kind of house would you like to be?

Blessings,

Abe, a River, and Cheetos

Good morning. I pray that the day finds you well.

I find myself swimming in the river behind my house a lot lately, almost every day. Actually, I do more standing in the river than swimming, since I usually have a bag of Cheetos cheese puffs in my hand.

Abe, my dog, does not like water, but he loves Cheetos cheese puffs.

Abe is a bassidor retriever, a name I gave him when I first saw him at the rescue shelter nine years ago. Abe is half basset hound, half golden retriever, and half something else.

One of the things that I love about being a theologian is that I don't have to worry about math.

Normally, Abe stays well away from water. I guess the golden part is overruled by the basset part. But if I get into the river with a bag of Cheetos, all bets are off. As soon as I enter the river, Abe is right next to me, paddling with his big basset feet and waiting for a cheese puff. Laurie goes down river about twenty yards with a handful of puffs, and Abe swims back and forth, eating them.

It is quite fun. I like to watch Abe swim. He is really good at it.

Abe likes his cheese puff–swim game.

When I come home from the YMCA, Abe meets me at the door all excited. He leads me to the pantry and barks until I retrieve the bag of puffs. Then he takes me to the bedroom, where my swimsuit is. He waits for me to put on my river shoes. Then he runs to the river, waiting for his puffs.

I get in the river, and swim time is on.

It has been fun watching Abe get over his fear of water. Something must have caused this fear when he was a pup.

The water is cold and clear in the river behind our house. I can see Abe paddling when he swims. His stroke is not anxious or hurried. It is a slow, powerful stroke. He actually likes to let the current take him, stroking only occasionally. He is relaxed.

As I stood in the river yesterday, watching Abe, my thoughts turned to Christ. He can take us to places, confront us with our fears, and show us that with Him we can overcome the things that inhibit us and live fearless lives.

I am reminded of something He told us. "Jesus looked at them and said, 'With man it is impossible, but not with God. For all things are possible with God'" (Mark 10:27 ESV).

Father, thank You for loving me. Thank You being there with me during the scary times. Thank You for getting into the water first and showing me it is okay by saying, "Come on in. The water is just fine." Thank You for being gentle when I doubt You or when I respond, "I don't know if I can do this." Thank You for encouraging and empowering me when I am weak and think a task is impossible. I love You. Amen.

Blessings,
Roger

The Little River behind My House

Good morning. I pray that the day finds you well.

I was standing in the river with Abe again this weekend. Go figure.

I like rivers. The water moves in rivers.

Ponds are nice. Lakes are cool.

Rivers are awesome.

Ponds are nice to laze around in and by. Lakes are fun if you have a boat.

Rivers are special. Rivers move.

The little river behind my house is not big, nor is it deep. The water is crystal clear. The river has a rocky bottom with differing depth holes in it. You can sit up to your waist in some holes. In others, you can sit up to your chest; in still others, you will be in over your head.

As I was standing in the river with Abe, a leaf floated by. I watched as it went one way, then another. Sometimes it would spin gently in the current; other times it would come to a rapid and careen through the torrent of water. Once it was through the rapid, it would come to a pool of slow-moving water and spin gently once again.

I saw a metaphor for life in this leaf floating down the river behind my house. Life has moments of calm when everything seems to be in order. Then the current speeds up. At first we do not notice. Then events go faster and faster. Sometimes we suddenly find ourselves in the rapids, and it is hard to see when they will end. Then we emerge from the rapids and enter a gentle pool where we can spin slowly and take life in. The process tends to repeat itself as we go through life. No two rapids are the same, but they are rapids nonetheless.

My thoughts turned to formation and transformation.

Formation and transformation in Christ are more like a river and less like a pond or a lake.

Formation and transformation in Christ are not stagnant processes; they involve constant movement.

We are not sitting in one place. We are either moving toward Christ or away from Him.

We are either forming and being transformed into Christ's likeness or we are forming and being transformed into something not like Him.

We are not sitting still. We are on the river of life.

I must always ask myself which way I am forming.

Father, as I travel down the river of life, help me. It is easy to contemplate You in the gentle motion of the slow water. I ask that You help me see You in the rapids too. As I endeavor to keep my focus on You, Lord, give me nudges when my attention drifts. I have been saved by Your grace. Help me to grow in You. Amen.

Blessings,
Roger

Fly-Fishing and Ministry

Good morning. I pray that the day finds you well.

My wife Laurie and I moved to a nice little house on a river about a year ago.

Since then, I have had this romantic idea of catching a steelhead. It is an amazing fish that I hear is a lot of fun to catch. I say I *hear* because I have never caught one!

I am a fly-fisherman. For those of you who are not fishermen, fly-fishing is not fishing for flies; it is a method of fishing in which an artificial fly is cast by use of a fly rod. If you want to know more about fly-fishing, watch the movie *A River Runs through It.*

I picture myself getting up in the morning, grabbing my gear, going to the river, catching a steelhead, taking a picture of my catch, then letting it go. The nice thing about fishing is that you do not have to kill a fish to have fun. But I like to eat fish, so I am sure there will be times when I bring one home for dinner, though even saying this sounds slightly barbaric.

Since we moved into the house, I have thought about finding all my stuff and going fishing. I spent the last few days opening boxes and going through them. I found all my gear and started making plans.

I say I have a romantic idea of catching a steelhead, because it takes an average of a thousand casts to land one. In reality, I will be on the river, strategizing, picking my spot, and casting, casting, casting. Finally, too tired to cast anymore, I will pack up my gear and come home empty-handed.

Ministry is a lot like fly-fishing for steelhead.

When you first enter ministry, you have a romantic notion that you will have a powerful impact, gaining tangible rewards that can be easily measured.

In reality, ministry is much harder. In reality, ministry is much dirtier. In reality, ministry can hurt.

As you spend more and more time in ministry, you either begin to see success in the small things or continue to feel defeated and ultimately burn out trying to achieve what others define as success.

It has been my experience with Christ that He is not impressed with the big deal. Christ asks us to be in daily relationship with Him and through this connection come into relationship with those who enter our lives, whoever they may be. We can then help them to see Him.

Ministry and fly-fishing are a lot alike. Both require many, many casts for a few fish.

The whole time I am fly-fishing, I am talking with God. The whole time I am with someone, God is talking with me.

As I go through my day, I will continue to find peace in the fact that God is using me to help people for His sake.

As you go through your day, measure your success in the little things and take peace in the fact that God is using you to help people for His sake.

Blessings,
Roger

Cheese, Crackers, PowerBait, and Unhealthy Spirituality

Good morning. I pray that the day finds you well.

I caught a fish Saturday—a trout, my favorite fish to catch. I am sure that a steelhead will become my favorite fish to catch if I ever catch one!

Laurie, Abe (my dog), and I made an afternoon of it.

We found a nice spot where I could fish, Laurie could sit and read, and Abe could snoofer. Abe is half basset hound and half golden retriever, and he loves snoofering. This involves doing dog stuff like putting his nose to the ground and following a scent.

Laurie brought all sorts of picnic supplies: sandwich fixings, cheese and crackers—the normal picnic stuff.

One of the tricks of the trade when fly-fishing is to put a small amount of PowerBait on the hook. There are several thoughts behind doing this. One thought is that it hides the hook; another is that it smells good to fish. I am of the second opinion. PowerBait smells terrible to me, so it must smell good to fish.

PowerBait comes in a jar and is gooey, smelly, and sticky. You dip your finger into the jar, take a small amount, and wipe it on the hook, making a tiny ball.

It seems to work, so I use it.

After fishing for some time and catching one trout (I let it go), I settled in for the picnic.

I was eating cheese and crackers when I noticed that my fingers were red—the same red as the PowerBait. While dipping my finger into the PowerBait jar, I had also noticed a warning label that read, "Not for Human Consumption!"

I wondered if I would get sick eating cheese and crackers and PowerBait. I thought about washing my hands, but that wasn't something a manly fisherman would do.

I decided that I would continue to eat my cheese and crackers and PowerBait.

As the afternoon wore on, Laurie and Abe and I were having a great time. Laurie and I talked about what the rest of the day would bring and about going to church on Sunday.

I did not make it to church on Sunday.

By the time I went to bed, my stomach wasn't feeling so hot. By 1:00 a.m., I was not feeling well at all. My body was trying to get rid of something by any means necessary.

I was sick.

Another way of saying I was sick is to say I was unhealthy.

As I lay in bed, a still small voice said, "This is what unhealthy spirituality is."

I said, "What?"

The voice continued, "This is what happens when people think they don't have to cut something unhealthy out of their lives. They come to Me, and I say, 'Don't do that anymore or don't think that way anymore.' And people say to themselves, *This won't hurt me. Even though Christ is telling me to cut this or that out of my life, this isn't so bad.* It is the same thinking that led you to believe you could leave the PowerBait on your fingers when you ate the cheese and crackers. The cheese and crackers were good; the PowerBait was bad. It took only a little PowerBait to turn everything bad, and now you are too sick to go to church. A long time ago, I told a story to another group of people about this very thing. This is what I said when I was asked what the kingdom of God is like. 'It is like the yeast a woman used in making bread. Even though she put only a little yeast in three measures of flour, it permeated every part of the dough.' The same thing happens with sin; it takes only a little to ruin the whole batch."

When you touch something that takes your focus off of Christ, wash your hands of it.

Unhealthy spirituality is not good.

Don't become a victim of a PowerBait episode.

Blessings,
Roger

Things My Grandfather Taught Me

Good morning. I pray that the day finds you well.

I was talking with a friend last night about Christmas, aging parents, and family in general. During the conversation I was reminded of my grandfather.

My grandfather retired and came to live with us on the farm when I was thirteen years old. Boppa, the name we had somehow known him by ever since I could remember, was a big man. He was tall, well-muscled, and generally pretty gruff. He wasn't a man to be trifled with. He grew up on the streets of Chicago during the twenties and thirties; he grew up tough.

In the early seventies, there were no places like Cabelas or GI Joes or the other sporting goods stores we know today. But there were mail-order outfits like LL Bean. Boppa loved to hunt and skeet shoot. He had all the gear, including a shooting shirt and a shooting vest complete with shoulder pad. He had a shooting hat and special hunting boots. He even had a very expensive skeet shotgun.

When my grandfather first came to live with us, I asked him, "Boppa, do you want to go skeet shooting?"

He replied, "Yes!"

I said, "Okay, get your stuff and let's go." I told my dad that I would need his help and that he should get his shotgun. It must have taken Boppa an hour to get ready. We piled into the pickup truck, the normal mode of transportation in Kansas, and we could hardly fit with all of

Boppa's gear. I climbed behind the wheel. (Kids learn to drive early on the farm.) So there we were. I was peeking through the spokes of the steering wheel, Dad was in the middle, and Boppa was squished against the passenger door. When I saw him, I could not help but giggle. Boppa looked much like a Saint Bernard with his head hanging out of the window to catch the wind.

I drove us to an old wooden bridge, stopping about one hundred yards short of it, and told my father and my grandfather to get out. Dad and Boppa looked at me, not really trusting my intentions, but grabbed their stuff and complied. I told Dad to walk softly to the middle of the bridge and to stand by the left guardrail. I told Boppa to walk softly to the middle of the bridge and to stand by the right guardrail. I walked to the middle of the bridge and stood in the middle of the road. When everyone was set, I looked at Boppa and said, "When you are ready, say *pull.*"

Boppa looked at me over his shoulder, still not knowing what to expect. Though he didn't have his gun ready, he said, "Pull."

At that, I jumped up and down on the bridge as hard as I could. From under the bridge more than a hundred pigeons flew out every which way. Boppa stood fumbling with his gun and screaming, "Oh, oh, oh my God! I wasn't ready!"

It wasn't long before everyone in town was talking about this old guy they saw jumping up and down on the country bridges, shooting at pigeons. It was quite a sight.

The years passed and I went to college and eventually joined the navy. I was at navigators school in Florida and had a few minutes, so I called home. Boppa answered the phone and he was the only one home. We talked about life; we talked about the farm; we talked about going skeet shooting. When it was time to hang up, I felt a strong urge to say, "Boppa, you know I love you." But we were not that kind of family. We didn't use the L-word much. So I didn't and we hung up.

The next morning the Red Cross got me out of class to inform me that Boppa had died the previous night of a major heart attack.

I learned something that day. I learned that life is fragile. I learned that things can change in an instant. I learned not to put off till tomorrow the important things that I could do today.

I started telling people how much they meant to me.

I started telling them how much I appreciated them.

I started telling people that I loved them.

I tell God that I love Him too.

Something to think about.

Blessings,
Roger

Simplexity

Good morning. I pray that the day finds you well.

Simplexity.

I wish that I had made up this word, but I didn't. I read it in a book.

I looked up *simplexity* in the dictionary, and this is what I found: "The word you've entered isn't in the dictionary." So I entered *simplex* in the dictionary, and this is what I found:

"Simplex (noun) a spatial configuration of *n* dimensions determined by *n* + 1 points in a space of dimension equal to or greater than *n* <a triangle together with its interior determined by its three vertices is a two-dimensional *simplex* in the plane or any space of higher dimension>."[5]

This definition doesn't put the cookies on the bottom shelf. Unless you are a mathematician, the wording tends to make you go, "Huh?"

So I looked up *simplex* as an adjective, and this is what I found:

"Simplex (adjective) Allowing telecommunication in only one direction <a *simplex* system>."

This is a definition that would satisfy a person who pontificates over the phone, but it doesn't explain what made me ponder the word as I read this book.

When I was thirteen years old, we moved to Kansas from a suburb of Chicago. Spending my first thirteen years in Chicago formed me

---

[5] http://www.merriam-webster.com/dictionary/simplex viewed June 6, 2012.

in certain ways. We did not talk to strangers, and we always walked to school in a group (when we were not dropped off by our parents in front of the school). People seemed to be in a hurry and were not very friendly. There seemed to be a lot going on; life felt rushed and complex.

Spending the rest of my growing-up years in Kansas formed me too, or perhaps reformed me.

My parents rented a farmhouse fourteen miles from town. Before moving in, we stayed briefly at a motel. On our first night there, Mom said, "I cannot believe that there are no taxis here."

I said, "Mom, why do we need a taxi? We can walk across the town in less than five minutes."

When we ventured out of the motel the following morning, I learned that our new hometown was quite different from our old one.

I noticed that everyone waved at us. At first we thought that something was wrong with our car and that people were trying to alert us. We did not wave back. We would stop the car and look it over, never finding anything wrong. People smiled when they waved, but frowned when we didn't wave back. After a while, we realized that we were supposed to return the greeting. It was like saying hello.

I noticed that drivers at intersections would not pull out into the street if a car was coming down the block. In Chicago, drivers pulled out in front of other cars all the time. If there was room to enter traffic, they went. We quickly discovered that pulling out in front of a car in this small town was a very rude thing to do. "What's the hurry?" people would say. In fact, I often wondered why people drove at all, since the town was so tiny.

We learned to wave.

We learned to wait.

We learned that this seemingly simple place had a complexity all its own.

Simplexity is the seemingly simple combined with the seemingly complex.

I like the definition from the book:

"There are two words I wish I had invented but didn't: *glocal* and *simplexity*. Like the word *glocal,* which brings together the global and the local, *simplexity* yokes the simple and the complex. The mystery of simplexity is the complex embracing the simple and the rational embracing the imcomprehensible."[6]

Our life with and in Christ is filled with simplexity.

Conversion is simple. It takes only a moment.

Transformation is complex. It takes a lifetime.

Asked to name the greatest commandment, Jesus said, "'Love the Lord your God with all your heart and with all your soul and with all your mind and with all your strength.' The second is this: 'Love your neighbor as yourself.' There is no commandment greater than these" (Mark 12:30–31).

It's simple; simply love.

It's complex; what does love look, taste, and feel like?

Our lives are filled with simplexity.

Our faith is filled with simplexity.

Let us be at peace with this fact. Let us be at peace with the mystery of living our simple lives confronted with the complexity of the higher dimension. Let us not be content with what we already know. Let us be filled with the wonder of a child and allow Christ to teach us at a deeper, higher plane.

Blessings,
Roger

---

[6] Leonard Sweet, *Viral* (Colorado Springs: WaterBrook Press, 2012), 44.

The ZipStrip Incident of 1976

Good morning. I pray that the day finds you well.

I woke up this morning to the pitter-pat of rain. I was cozy in my bed and thought how wonderful it was to be snuggly warm with rain falling softly on the roof.

That is when I realized that Laurie and I had moved all the stuff from the garage outside to prepare for an inspection.

A few days ago we received an e-mail stating that a code official wanted to look at the garage and that we needed to move our "stuff" outside so that the inspection could take place. The e-mail went on to say that the garage could not be properly inspected because of all our "stuff." I responded that we would be happy to comply and that we were more than willing to move our "stuff" outside for the event. I pointed out that the "stuff" was our belongings and that we would rather put our "stuff" outside on a sunny day. After much back-and-forth, the inspection was scheduled for today, since the weather reports showed sunshine. Last night Laurie and I moved our "stuff." I keep putting *stuff* in quotation marks because I found the inspector's use of the term more than a little insensitive.

The e-mail could have said, "We would like to inspect your garage. We will not be able to do a thorough inspection because of the limited access that we have. If you would be willing to help us by moving your belongings to a temporary location for the inspection, we would greatly appreciate it."

When I was a kid growing up in Kansas, my dad would take on projects that appeared to have a low chance of success. Here is a short list of things he tackled:

- Red, an old Appaloosa horse that had been foundered. The term *foundered* is used to describe a horse that has become lame because its hooves have grown so long that it must walk on the frogs of its feet. I won't go into what frogs are, but suffice it to say Red could not walk. Dad bought him, and we carried him into the trailer and brought him home. I thought Dad was nuts.
- Changing a duplex into one large home.
- Stucco, a lath and plaster system for ceilings and walls. What did people use before the invention of drywall? Stucco.
- Installing a hot-water heating system all by himself.

One day I walked in as Dad was stripping paint from one of the windowsills of our duplex-turned-huge house. He turned to me and said, "Do me a favor and go to Milton's and get some ZipStrip." Milton's was the lumberyard in town. It was named after Milton Lampe, the guy who owned it. It was also known as Lampe Hardware. Most of the shops in our little town were named after people. I had learned over time, mostly from the red-handled screwdriver incident of 1974, to ask clarifying questions.

I asked, "How much ZipStrip do you need?"

Dad, obviously frustrated, said, "You know how much I need. Just go get me some blankety-blank ZipStrip." So I drove the pickup to Milton's.

I walked into the office and said, "I need all the ZipStrip you can spare."

Seeing that I was more than a little tweaked, Milton said, "What's going on, Roger?" I recounted the story and told him my plan. Milton laughed and said, "Let's go to the warehouse." We loaded all the ZipStrip that he had, everything from pint cans to five-gallon buckets.

Milton said, "Just bring back what you don't need, and tell me how it goes."

I returned to the house and I walked in with a pint can of ZipStrip. Dad, who had cooled off while I was gone, said, "Thank you."

I said, "No problem," and went back to the pickup to unload the rest. Dad watched in fascination as I brought in enough ZipStrip to strip the paint on every house in town. A smile came to his face and he said he was sorry for overreacting to a simple question, especially after the red-handled screwdriver incident of 1974.

Dad even went with me to Lampe Hardware to return the unneeded ZipStrip. Milton had a good laugh. Dad thought it was pretty funny too.

I remembered the ZipStrip incident of 1976 as I read the e-mail about our "stuff." The thought occurred to me that I might find some way to make the inspector pay for his insolence. But I am much older now and have hopefully learned a little during my life.

One of the benefits of memorizing Scripture is that passages come to mind when you face life's situations. This verse seems appropriate now:

"A kind man benefits himself, but a cruel man brings trouble on himself" (Prov. 11:17).

Laurie and I ran outside and covered everything with tarps.

We are grateful that the inspection is being done.

We are thankful that Christ is in our lives.

Christ gives us the ability to see things differently and not to get upset over trivialities.

I thank God that through Christ there will not be another ZipStrip-style incident.

Blessings,
Roger

A Chicken Named Pit Silo

Good morning. I pray that the day finds you well.

We have family in town and we are still getting settled into our new home; I know this is not an excuse, but I guess I am looking for one and this is what I came up with.

Many of you have responded to "The ZipStrip Incident of 1976" Bread. I like all the conversation. Some of you seem to be interested in the red-handled screwdriver incident of 1974. I will get around to that one soon.

This morning I started thinking about my favorite chicken.

Back on the farm, we had many chickens, geese, a rather strange one-eyed duck, guinea hens, horses, a pet pig, sheep, cats, and two dogs. The farm had a corral, a barn, two cattle/horse pens, and an area in which sheep or pigs could reside if they were so inclined. We also had a chicken coup. Our farm was more of a petting zoo, and all the animals regarded themselves as part of the family. I think this was because we were not real farmers but people who liked living on a farm.

We also had a pit silo.

A pit silo is a silo that goes down instead of up. A silo is the tall, cylindrical structure that you might spot if you are driving in the country. If it is blue, it is a Harvester silo, one of the expensive ones. Everybody wanted a Harvester silo and a John Deere tractor, but not everyone could get them.

A pit silo is just like those tall, above-ground silos, but it is dug into the ground. Our pit silo was made of concrete. I am not sure how deep it went. There was always silage in it. Silage is chopped-up cornstalks and other stuff that cattle like to eat. I am glad that cattle like to eat silage, because I don't think it tastes very good. Yes, I have tried it. Fortunately, since cattle find it so appetizing, Mom did not feed it to us.

We had a chicken named Pit Silo. She was rather ugly, as chickens go. She seemed to be in a constant state of molting. Pit Silo was very healthy, but the bald patches made her look unwell and rather scary. We called her Pit Silo because she liked to nest right next to this structure. She had the annoying habit of laying an egg, jumping up excitedly, and promptly falling into the silo.

One of my jobs on the farm was to get her out of the pit silo. The silage was always around twenty feet down from the top. I had to climb down a ladder inside the silo and chase a chicken. Dad would lower a metal pail on a rope, and after I put the chicken in the pail, he would haul the pail up and remove the chicken. Then he would tell me to get out of the pit before the fumes overcame me.

I learned three things on my first foray into the pit silo.

First, the silo was round. Try cornering a chicken in a space that has no corners.

Second, there were pockets in the silage. I could be running along, take my next step, and be gone. Luckily, I sank only up to my chest, Still this was a bit unsettling.

Third, the silage fermented. I think that is why cattle liked it so much; feeding time was probably cattle happy hour. The fermentation produced gases that ate up oxygen, and this could lead to suffocation. I was always worried about suffocating and even more concerned about the funeral that would follow. As I chased a chicken around the silo—chickens are fast, by the way—I kept thinking about the eulogy. "Roger died chasing a chicken around a pit silo. He suffocated on fermented cornstalks." This would be an embarrassing way for a fourteen-year-old boy to go.

Eventually I would catch the chicken, and as time passed Pit Silo did not run from me. She would lay her egg, get excited, fall into the silo, and wait patiently for me to come pick her up and place her gently in the metal pail. Dad would pull her to freedom, and I would climb out.

As a result of this ritual, Pit Silo became quite tame. She would come up on the porch and would jump right into the lap of anyone sitting there. She thought of herself as a pet. The real farmers would come over and shake their heads at these people sitting on the porch with a featherless chicken on one lap, a cat on another, a dog resting on the porch, and a pig lying on its back on the lawn.

My office here at the YMCA is right by the welcome center. I listen to the conversations as people come in. Many conversations are about lives that resemble my chasing a chicken in a pit silo. What I love about our welcome center is that after listening to these gripes, which are actually cries for help, our staff tells people that the Y is a place to let the world flow off their backs.

People come to work out.

They come to sit and to read.

They come to decompress.

We are welcoming community of people who are more interested in what a person looks like on the inside than on the outside. We look past pit silos and see the beauty of the heart within.

Pit Silo eventually learned not to fall into the pit. Her feathers grew in, and she was as beautiful on the outside as she was on the inside.

We see the same thing here at the YMCA. People heal inside and become healthy, which shows on the outside too.

If you have not been to a YMCA lately, check it out. Chances are there is a place for you.

"I do not ask for these only, but also for those who will believe in me through their word, that they may all be one, just as you, Father, are in me, and I in you, that they also may be in us, so that the world may believe that you have sent me." (John 17:20–21).

I look forward to seeing you.

Blessings,
Roger

The Case of the Empty Coffee Cup

Good morning. I pray that the day finds you well.

I will sometimes sit with people who are going through a particularly hard time. The problem often involves a transition of one sort or another. During these sessions, I do a lot of listening. People are looking for answers that I do not have. They always ask why.

Life on the farm was very different from life today. The pace was much slower although we did not realize it at the time. We learned to wait.

One early October day, we decided to take a family picture. We did not hire a professional photographer. We took the picture ourselves. That is how one does things on the farm.

It was a brisk day and we all wore coats. We lined up in front of the house. Boppa, our photographer, stood in front of us, giving us directions: move to the right; move to left; Katie, stop making faces. You know the drill.

Mom held her coffee. She had her favorite cup. When I was a kid there was no such thing as a travel mug with a lid.

We all had ceramic mugs with our favorite pictures on them. We got used to drinking only a portion of what was in our cups, since most of it was jostled out before we could finish. When somebody showed up with a traveler's mug for the first time, most people said, "This is simply ingenious. I should have thought of this. I could have made a fortune."

But we were too busy to invent a traveler's mug.

We were too busy spilling our drinks, complaining about spilling our drinks, and going to get more. With all that happening, who had time to invent anything? Mom's cup carried a picture of a chicken. I think it was a Rhode Island Red. It most definitely was not Pit Silo. A coffee mug with a picture of Pit Silo would not have improved the drinking experience at all.

Just as Boppa was getting ready to take the picture with his Instamatic camera, Tinker, one of our horses, wandered into the frame. She was loose on the farm. Half Shetland pony and half quarter horse, she was part of the family and tended to be wherever we were. Now Boppa had a completely new set of instructions to give us.

Finally, he said, "Cheese." (I have always thought this was a funny thing to say, but that is just me.) Boppa took the shot and the flash went off.

If you are under forty-five, you probably do not remember the Instamatic camera with the magnesium flashcubes. I believe these cubes were responsible for early-onset retinal blindness. Every time one of them went off everyone would wander around seeing nothing but dots.

I am sure that some alien watching would think, *What a weird ceremony!* People would smile and stand very still. Then a bright light would go off and these people would wander around with their hands out in front of them, bumping into each other and inanimate objects.

I am surprised that some attorney (I apologize in advance to all my attorney friends reading this) has not brought a class-action lawsuit. I can see the commercial now. "If you or your family members have ever had your picture taken with an Instamatic camera with a magnesium flashcube, you may be entitled to a cash reward. Having a picture taken with an Instamatic camera with a magnesium flashcube has been linked to rentinalmiophlagination, a disease associated with seeing dots and bumping into other people."

When the picture had been taken and we could see again, Mom went to take a drink of coffee from her chicken cup. It was empty and she was mystified.

Back in the old days, we did not have digital cameras. We used film.

An Instamatic was not so instant after all. A typical roll might have thirty-five shots on it.

After you take a family picture, you want to see it as soon as possible. I now realize where all those pictures that make you go "hmm" come from. When you took a set of pictures with an old-fashioned camera, there were usually a few shots left on the roll. You could not send in a partial roll of film and waste those leftover possibilities, so you shot the rest of the roll, then paid for the pictures to be processed. Such thinking is another clue as to why we never invented the traveler's mug. I will often see a stack of pictures with really cool shots at the top. Then toward the end there will be three or four pictures of Dad asleep on the couch, mouth agape, arms splayed out, and one leg on the floor. Those are the pictures from the end of the roll.

We would finish a roll and leave the film at a store in town. The store would send the film to Goodland or to Denver or to another place that had the magical film-processing machine. The place would process the film and send it back to our store, and we would pick up the pictures. This could take up to three weeks.

When we got the family pictures back, complete with Dad asleep on the couch, the case of the missing coffee was solved.

When Boppa took the shot, Tinker, standing right behind Mom, leaned over gently and carefully and stuck her tongue into the chicken mug, slurping up all the coffee without anyone noticing.

We had a nice family picture complete with a horse's tongue in a chicken cup.

Often, when I sit with people who are asking why, I know that we do not have the answer at that moment. As time passes, God will eventually let us see glimpses of why. If we submit to Him, Christ can use us to help others who are going through what we once endured.

As much as we would like to think otherwise, we do not live in an Instamatic world, and our faith walk is a marathon, not a sprint.

As I have grown in my relationship with Christ, I have learned to be patient. I have learned to be less interested in knowing right now and am content with knowing that Christ loves us and loves me, and that no matter what happens He is with us and with me.

Blessings,
Roger

Ice-skating the Great Republican River

Good morning,

I pray the day finds you well.

The river behind my house has ice on it. It is not iced over, the temperature is not nearly cold enough for that, but it has ice on it non-the-less. As I stood in my back yard looking at the river, a memory came to mind, a memory from the early 70's.

Growing up in St. Francis Kansas we had a river that flowed close to town, it was called the Great Republican River.

Bob Sperry, Tim Raile, and I decided to go ice-skating on the Great Republican River. I know this sounds dangerous but really, it was not, or so we thought.

You see the Great Republican River had been dammed in the late 30's after a particularly devastating flood. At least that is what we were told. The unintended consequence of this damming of the Great Republican River was that the river was no longer Great. The river had been reduced to a trickle at best and spent most of the summers rather dry.

But, this was not summer, it was winter and there was more water in the river. The water was also frozen.

So Tim, Bob and I decided to go ice-skating. One might ask themselves why three kids from Kansas would have ice-skates; one might ask that question. Of course, one might ask why we had snow ski's, or an old parachute but then one never knows when something will come in handy.

We went down by the grain elevator, which if you are not from the country might be a little confusing. A grain elevator is exactly what it sounds like, it elevates the grain. I never really understood why grain needed to be elevated, I guess carbohydrates have poor self esteem, and needs to be lifted up. I know that grain has a bad temper, at least that is what I have been told. The grain elevator operators always told us to be careful around grain elevators, grain elevators tended to explode. Evidently, smoking really upset carbohydrates. I had heard of a guy who was smoking in a grain elevator once and the whole thing blew up, nasty tempers those carbohydrates have.

We went down to the grain elevator, which was by the Great Republican River. We put on our skates and quickly fell through the ice. We fell through all the way up to our ankles. We stepped out of the river, back onto the ice, and were on our way. It was quite an adventure really. Skating up river, jumping the sandbars, dodging the unfrozen parts. The river is really pretty in the winter and from the vantage point of the ice everything seemed different.

We skated for quite a while. We skated all the way out to the Riverside Golf Course. We skated to the pond that was at the golf course. The pond was frozen over too.

We had a blast.

After a little while, Bob made a mistake and took off his gloves. That is when we noticed he did not have any color in his fingers. Everything was fine and dandy until Bob took off his gloves. Immediately we got scared. Thoughts of losing our fingers to frostbite came rushing into our heads and out of our mouths. Once we started down that road, it was a short hop-skip-and-a-jump too wild wolves, mountain lions, and our parents finding our bodies on the bank of the river come springtime. It did not matter that we were no longer on the river. It did not matter that we were fifteen minutes from town. It did not matter that we had never seen a wolf or a mountain lion.

I have often wondered who thought these things up, I think it was Bob he was the smart one.

We gathered sticks to make a fire. We did not have any matches, nor did we have a lighter. None of us smoked, to afraid of upsetting the local carbohydrates. Tim, who we used to call wilderness man. We didn't actually call him that but looking back we should have. Anyway, Tim grabs one of the sticks and starts to roll it back and forth in his hands the way wilderness men do to make a fire. He never made a fire but what we quickly noticed was all this fire making work warmed our hands up quickly.

As what usually happens with young boys, we got bored, we started to get hungry, and we skated home, making a wide birth around the grain elevator.

Looking back on some of our adventures it is impossible to see that God was not right there with us skating down the river. He showed us many wonderful things; He shared His creation with us. I am sure that He laughed when our imaginations went wild. I had not thought about our ice-skating adventure for many years until today. Thank you Father for reminding me that you want us to enjoy life and that it is an adventure.

My prayer is:

Father, continue to show me things. Continue to nudge me into adventures, while at the same time reminding me of the adventures that You had given me already.

Blessings,
Roger

You call me out upon the waters.

Good morning,

I pray the day finds you well.

You call me out upon the waters.

Growing up in northwest Kansas was a lot of fun. We had T.V.'s but only one station; obviously, this was before the time of satellite T.V., ComCast, Frontier, and all those cable companies. It was before computers, the internets, and WWW.//////# and all that stuff.

What we did have was horses, motorcycles, pickup trucks, tractors, and a boat. Actually, I had the horses, a motorcycle it was an orange Yammerhammer 125 Enduro, and a pickup truck, a green and white 1966 Ford F-150. Tim had the tractors, a John Deere 4020, a John Deere 4630, and a 1936 John Deere –G. Tim also had a pick-up truck; it was a GMC with a toolbox bolted onto the bed. The boat also belonged to Tim. It was an Orange Glastron. Actually, none of us owned any of that stuff, our parents did, but as kids, we thought it was ours as well.

The Great Republican River ran right by our little town, but since it was dammed in the 1930's it really wasn't much of a river anymore. The dam created a lake though. It was called Bonnie Lake, for that matter, the dam was called Bonnie Dam. The dam and the lake were actually in Colorado, which sounds as if it was far away. In all actuality, Bonnie Dam was a mere 20 miles or so. We lived right on the border of Kansas and Colorado. A note of interest; northeastern Colorado looks an awful lot like northwest Kansas.

One day, Tim, Bob, and I decided to take the boat to Bonnie Dam. Of course, this meant that we had to take the pickup too. We loaded up all our stuff and headed to the lake. Tim was a very accomplished water-skier. He could slalom ski, which always left us impressed. The only time I was on one ski was when the water had just ripped the other one off and I was about to get a face full of lake water or worse.

You call me out upon the waters.

Bob was not much of a water-skier at all. In fact, he had never gotten up on skis before. Today, we decided that Bob would learn how to water-ski.

The lake had little wind waves on it. The wind tends to blow in Kansas, for that matter, the wind tends to blow in eastern Colorado too, not much difference. We experienced boaters called the lake "choppy."

Bob would get into position, his ski-tips up and facing the boat, yell, "Hit-it" and we would throttle up the boat.

Bob would come most of the way out of the water, bent at the waist with his nose almost touching his toes, arms stretched out straight. Just when we thought he would get up on top of the water and ski he would start to wobble; the wobble becoming more pronounced until he would fall back into the water. He kept a death grip on the towline and we would always have to yell, "Let go." I was afraid we were going to drown Bob.

The water was "choppy. Bob's line of sight reduced to a few feet when he bobbed (no pun intended) in the water.

You call me out upon the waters.

A funny phenomenon occurred that day. Bonnie Dam had many critters that called the lake home. There were deer, coyotes, rabbits, snakes, all sorts of land creatures. Bob was not concerned with land creatures at that moment he was in the water. Bonnie Dam had trout, bass, bluegills carp, and catfish. We had grown up with horror stories of giant catfish that would grab people and eat them. I do not think any of these stories are true, but back when I was a kid we thought about catfish a lot when we were in the lake.

The funny phenomenon was that as the water temperature heated up in the lake it became hypoxic. Hypoxia is when the oxygen levels in the water become low. In itself, hypoxia is not funny, what was funny was that carp, a family of fish that tend to grow large in lakes. The Carp come to the surface and gulp air when the oxygenation of the water falls below certain levels.

The water was "choppy." The carp were coming to the surface. Bob was bobbing. We saw the carp coming. We kept asking Bob if he was ready to try again. Bob kept saying, "Not yet." Then it happened.

You call me out upon the waters.

A wave came and went, and right behind the wave was a great big "Killer" carp. Bob started beating the carp with one hand and yelling, "Hit-it, Hit-it." Bob came right up out of the water.

He was skiing. It was the most amazing thing I ever saw. A one-handed start. A start with Bob still looking behind him to see if any "Killer Carp" were still chasing him.

You call me out upon the waters.

When I think about growing up in Kansas, I cannot help but see God in the middle of those years.

I also think about when God calls us out upon the waters, He takes us from a place that we perceive ourselves to be safe, to a place of unknown, to a place that takes us out of our comfort zone. It is only then that we have the opportunity to see what we can really do.

Father, continue to call me out upon the waters. Continue to stretch and remake me as I do my best to grow in your image. Forgive my failings as I forgive others who have failed me. Lead me father. Lead me out upon the waters.

Blessings,
Roger

The great unknown
where feet may fail

Good morning,

I pray the day finds you well.

Growing up I had a best friend named Tim. Tim used to take me water-skiing a lot.

Tim was a great water-skier. I was not.

I eventually learned to water ski with one ski. I should rephrase this; I eventually learned to stay on top of the water for more than fifteen seconds on one ski that is more accurate.

Tim however, could do many amazing things.

One of the coolest things Tim did was have the boat bring him in close to shore, Tim would let go of the rope. He would glide over the top of the water with the greatest of ease. When he got to the shore, he would simple step out of the ski and stand on the beach.

I wanted to do this so bad it hurt, because it was so cool.

One day, a whole crowd of us were at Bonnie Dam. When I say a whole crowd, I mean a lot of us. When I say a lot of us there must have been at least ten or twelve. You might not think that ten or twelve teenagers is a lot of people but going up in northwest Kansas, more specifically Cheyenne County, Kansas ten or twelve teens was a lot.

Cheyenne County is located in the Norwest corner of Kansas. It covers roughly 1,022 square miles; back when I lived in Cheyenne

County there were roughly 5,000 people that lived in the county. The little town that I grew up in, St. Francis had a population of roughly 1,800 people. This meant that while there were roughly 5,000 people in the county, 1,800 of them lived in town; leaving roughly 3,000 people to occupy the rest of the county. I will check my math later, but I think this only leaves around three people per square mile.

Anytime you had ten or twelve people in any one location, it was a crowd.

In this crowd, there was a bunch of girls. When I say, "A bunch of girls" I mean there were like four, or maybe even five girls in the crowd.

You might not think that four or even maybe five girls are a bunch of girls. If that is what you think, you obviously did not grow up in northwest Kansas.

Tim was busy showing off his water skiing prowess to the crowd on the shore. When he finished he let go of the rope, glided gracefully over the water, ski hitting the sand, Tim stepping gracefully out of the ski, walking up to the crowd of girls saying, "Hey." Evidently, "Hey" is a pretty cool thing to say once you have just stepped out of a slalom ski because it sure made the girls swoon.

I was busy trying to make a campfire. When you can't step out of a water-ski onto the beach and make the girls swoon just by saying, "Hey" you make a fire. Bob and I were making a fire. I was glad I had Bob to help me. I never could make a fire but Bob was good at chemistry, I guess that is why he is a doctor now, and had that whole fuel, oxygen, heat thing down pretty good.

I wanted to step out of a water-ski, say, "Hey", and make the girls swoon too. I wanted to do that so bad that I went up to Tim, who was still standing in front of the crowd of girls smiling his wry smile, and said, "Tim, will you take me water-skiing? Tim said, "Sure" and away we went.

The great unknown where feet may fail.

I took off with only one ski. I managed to stay up as I came out of the water. I even made a couple jumps over the wake, hoping some of the crowd would notice. Tim took me around the lake and then I signaled for him to take me to shore. As we came closer to shore, I could see Tim was yelling something but I could not make it out.

One of the things you do not want to do is let go of the rope too early. There is nothing more embarrassing than gliding to a halt still 20 yards from shore, sinking in the water as your momentum slowed, and then having to swim awkwardly to shore with a ski still attached to your foot. No, you do not want that to happen.

When I thought I was close enough to the shore to let go, glide gracefully over the water, and step out of the ski on the beach, I let go of the rope.

The great unknown where feet may fail.

At first, everything seemed to be going as planned. I was skimming over the water and I was sure I had enough energy to make to shore. In fact, the thought crossed my mind that I was going pretty fast.

As I got closer to the beach I realized a few things. First, that I was still going way too fast. Second, that I must not have let go of the rope soon enough. Third, things were not going to go as planned.

When I hit the shore I must have still been going about twenty miles an hour; I stepped out of the ski, well maybe it was more like being thrown out of the ski as the ski planted itself rather firmly in the sand. I tried to keep up with my feet, but could not. As my face headed quickly for the sand all I could think of to do was tuck and roll. I did that really well. I tucked and I rolled right through the campfire that Bob and I had just finished building before I went water-skiing.

I had been out skiing just long enough for the fire to take off and grow quite large. It was blazing away when I rolled through it. I came to a stop in front of the crowd of girls, hair smoldering, I through my arms out wide and said, "Ta-Da."

Nobody swooned.

After Tim parked the boat, he came over to check on me. I asked him what he was trying to tell me. He said that he could see that we were getting to close to the beach and he was yelling for me to let go of the rope.

The great unknown where feet may fail.

120

As I look back on my youth there are many instances where I tried to over execute. I tried to do things I had no business doing. If I had been more attentive to God, He would have given me the confidence to know that I did not have to water-ski on one ski, and slide into shore to be accepted and loved. Tim had a gift for this and it was cool to watch him do it. If I had been more attentive to God, I would not have had to go to a place where my feet failed. God, in His infinite wisdom, saw this as a teachable moment. What He taught me was even though I failed at water-skiing onto a beach I had many friends that cared about my wellbeing. People that loved me.

The great unknown where feet may fail.

I went to the great unknown where my feet did fail. What God showed me in this is that not only is He there with me but that it is better to try to fail than to never try at all.

Go into the great unknown.

Give God the opportunity to show you great things.

Blessings,
Roger

The Red-Handled Screwdriver
Incident of 1974

Good morning. I pray that the day finds you well.

Many people live by the old American Express slogan "Don't leave home without it."

For my father, "it" was a red-handled screwdriver. There was nothing extra special about this screwdriver. It carried a logo, something like Craftsman, but the logo was covered with paint blotches. It was a Standard-head with an eight-inch shaft, and it had a red handle.

My dad was always doing and redoing things around the house. The house was his hobby.

For most of us in farm country, a pair of pliers was the tool of choice. Not my dad. His tool of choice was the red-handled screwdriver. He used it for

- screwing in screws;
- making scratch marks on things when he measured;
- opening paint cans—thus the paint blotches;
- making the dent required before drilling a hole in something; and
- tapping a child (usually me) on the head when needed.

He always had his red-handled screwdriver with him when he was doing a project.

One day, Dad came into the house yelling, "Clare (my mom's name), Clare, Claaaaaaaaaaaaaaaare!"

Mom usually waited until Dad yelled, "Claaaaaaaaaaaaaaare," before answering. I think she did this to make sure that it was not a false alarm and that she was really needed. Or perhaps she liked hearing her name in an extended format.

Mom appeared around the corner. The bellowing had already brought the kids into the room. When Dad bellowed we would come running. It would be nice to say that this was out of reverence, but we were not all that well behaved. We usually came just to see what would transpire. Cable had not been invented, and we were still amazed at the traveler's mug invention, so this was a form of entertainment for us kids.

Mom said, "You do not need to bellow. (I always thought that she made this happen by waiting to answer.) What do you need, honey?"

Dad said, "I cannot find my red-handled screwdriver."

Mom asked, "Have you looked for it yet?" Obviously, she was privy to some of Dad's behavioral traits that we kids were not.

Dad said, "Of course I have."

He started to shout orders.

You need to read this next part out load, using a deep, authoritative voice much like General Patton would have used during the Battle of the Bulge.

"Kids, you look here. Clare, you look there. When you find it, let out a yell, letting the others know that you have it. I will do the same if I find it. We will all meet back here in fifteen minutes if we have not found it. Go!"

Okay. You can use your normal voice again.

Dad spun on his heals to go look, and that is when we found the red-handled screwdriver. It was sticking out of his back pocket. He had obviously grabbed it earlier and forgotten that he had it, then spent the next thirty minutes looking for it before he assembled the troops to look for it some more.

We had two options before us. We could tell Dad that his precious screwdriver was in his back pocket, or we could remain silent. For whatever reason, we chose option B and did not say a word.

Dad looked for another fifteen minutes, and we pretended to look for fifteen minutes. It would not have been much of a ruse if we had not pretended.

At the predetermined time, we reassembled in the staging area.

Dad was distraught over the loss of his screwdriver and was beginning to pout. This usually brought on the sandwich that made everything better.

That is when Katie said, "Look in your back pocket." Then she giggled. Katie giggles like Betty Rubble in *The Flintstones*. If you don't know how Betty Rubble giggles, watch an episode. Katie's giggle is spot-on.

Katie was the chosen spokesperson for our group. She could get away with things that the rest of us could not. It was like she had secret information on Dad that gave her immunity. I am not sure what this information was because the Ketchup Treaty of 1978 had not been established yet, but she had something. I am sure of it.

Dad looked in his back pocket, and sure enough there was his red-handled screwdriver.

Dad had become paralyzed without this screwdriver. He could not start a project without it, even though he had other screwdrivers and a bunch of other tools. This screwdriver had become so important to him that nothing else mattered at the time. It had become his idol.

Christ cautions us about being too attached to earthly things, warning that having an idol is a bad thing. He knows that if we get too attached to earthly things we focus on the wrong stuff, like a red-handled screwdriver. We spend our time looking and not doing.

Christ tells a parable about a man who found treasure in a field and sold everything he had so that he could buy the field and gain the treasure.

If we have Christ with us, in our back pocket, we spend our days focused on the things that He is focused on. If we cannot find Christ, "a dark night of the soul" experience, we must look for Him, and when we find Him, we must let go of everything else so that He can be our focus.

My prayer is that as we go through the day we recognize the red-handled screwdrivers in our lives and put them in their proper place, that we let them go and replace them with Christ.

Blessings,
Roger

Don't Put Your Date in the Trunk

Good morning. I pray that the day finds you well.

Being a chaplain entails many responsibilities, one of which is spiritual direction. Working with people in this capacity, I have the opportunity to get them to look through the hidden doors and the closed windows in their lives and on their spiritual journeys.

When I was growing up, we had a drive-in on the edge of town. Everything seemed to be on the edge of town. When we left the farm during my sophomore year in high school, we moved into a house on the north edge of town. The grain elevator was at the west end of town, three blocks away. The high school was at the east edge of town, six blocks away. The motel was at the south edge of town, ten blocks away. Our town was small.

I have mentioned that one of my favorite pastimes was to get up on Saturday morning to watch *The Bugs Bunny-Road Runner Hour* on TV. Not only was this one of my favorite programs, but it was one of the few programs that KLOE Goodland offered. I would get out of bed, go to the kitchen, and make a gallon of chocolate milk. My mother said that when I went away to college she could not get the milk delivery shut off fast enough. Yes, this was back in the days when milkmen delivered the milk in little white trucks. She said she was bathing in milk until she got the situation rectified.

I would bring the chocolate milk back downstairs, where the TV was located, and sit watching my cartoons, drinking contentedly. I didn't bother to put on any clothes; this was all done in my underpants.

My sisters used to love to collect things; they would bring home all sorts of things—stray dogs, cats, boys. Katie always had a crowd with her.

There I was enjoying my cartoons and my chocolate milk, and Katie would traipse into the room with all her friends. Great! Now I would have to go put clothes on. My day had just taken a turn for the worse.

One of Katie's best friends was Peggy. Because this was a small community, we all knew each other well. Unfortunately, Peggy was just one of many who had seen me in my underpants. One day I called Peggy up and asked her to go to the movies with me. It was summertime and this meant going to the drive-in.

I was nervous when I called. Her mother answered the phone. Why do moms always have to answer the phone when a boy wants to talk to a girl? It was disconcerting and intimidating to have to say, "Hello, Mrs. Peters, is Peggy there?" Peggy came to the phone, and all I could manage was, "Hi, Peggy. This is Roger. Want to go to the movies with me?"

Then there was the dreaded pause.

After an eternity, Peggy said yes.

We took care of the details—the time, the date, the movie.

The day arrived and I picked up Peggy and we drove to the drive-in. This was much better than walking to the drive-in, which would have been silly, or having my mother drive us there, which would have been embarrassing. I know. It happened.

One of the favorite local pastimes when going to the drive-in was to see how many friends you could get in for free.

This meant having a bunch of kids get into the trunk. Mrs. Edmundson, the owner of the drive-in, handled the ticket booth. She was really smart.

The driver would pull up to the booth and say, "One, please." Mrs. Edmundson would ask, "Where are all your friends?" The driver would say, "They are coming soon." Mrs. Edmundson's eyebrow would rise; when this happened the driver knew he was busted. She would say, "Let's take a look in the trunk." The driver would get out and open the trunk, and twenty or thirty kids would pile out. Actually, it was more like two or three, but it was always a theatrical experience when this happened.

I pulled up to the drive-in booth, and Mrs. Edmundson said, "Roger, where is Peggy? You do have a date with her tonight, don't you?"

Another attribute of a small town is that everybody knows everything about everybody.

I looked at Mrs. Edmundson sheepishly; her eyebrow was already raised. Not saying a word, I got out and opened the trunk.

Out popped Peggy.

Mrs. Edmundson said, "Really, Roger! You put your date in the trunk?"

I told you that Mrs. Edmundson was smart.

I found out two things that night. First, though Peggy was pretty and funny, taking her to the movies was like taking my sister. Our friendship was too good to mess it up by dating. Second, never put your date in the trunk. It is really bad form.

When I counsel people, I remember Mrs. Edmundson.

I do my best to get them to look into their trunks. I know that God is continually nudging me to look into my trunk, to open closed doors and windows as Christ walks with me.

Have you opened any doors or windows lately?

Blessings,
Roger

A Conversation about Heaven

Good morning. I pray that the day finds you well.

I have been doing a lot of thinking lately about God, Christ, the Holy Spirit, and heaven.

In the beginning was God.

As Christians, we believe in the Trinity. If we believe in the Trinity, we believe that God, Christ, and the Holy Spirit are one. If we believe that, we believe that God, Christ, and the Holy Spirit existed from the beginning. I know it's hard to wrap your head around this idea. The more you contemplate it, the deeper it gets, and frankly we see through the glass darkly and will never get the complete picture until we are with the Trinity. This means that we would be in heaven with God, Christ, and the Holy Spirit.

Being in heaven with God, Christ, and the Holy Spirit also is a lot to wrap your head around.

Many preachers and pastors have told us that heaven will be like a big banquet, with never-ending food and never-ending praise songs. I hope that heaven is more than just eating and singing. I do like to eat, thus the reason for my current weight loss endeavor. But as much as I like to eat, doing it for eternity would get old. I hope that we are not eating for eternity.

The more I think about the possibility, the more I wonder about it. First, wouldn't eating for eternity be gluttony? Isn't gluttony a sin? There is no sin in heaven. Second, there a multiple schools of thought about who will be in heaven. One school says that only the souls of people will gain admittance. Another school of thought has animals up in heaven too. (Countless pastors have been asked, "Will my cat Buffy be in heaven? It sure wouldn't be heaven if my cat Buffy isn't there.") Other schools of thought have souls from other worlds in heaven too. Heaven could be quite the place when you consider who could be there.

Let's stick with the second school of thought for now.

If all we do is eat, where will the food come from?

If we are in heaven, there is no reason to think that we could not communicate with animals. If all we do is eat, I can see a conversation like this:

Roger: "Hello, Cathy." (I am talking to Cathy the cow.)
Cathy: "Hello, Roger." (Cathy the cow is talking to me.)
Roger: "What are you doing today?"
Cathy: "Eating."
Roger: "Me too."
Cathy: "What are you eating today?"
Roger: "I am so glad you asked, because today I am in charge of the barbecue."

I do not think that Cathy the cow would think she was in heaven if she was a vital part of the banquet.

I was in my aqua aerobics class this morning as part of my weight loss endeavor. I was doing water walking, weights in hand, and was obviously lost in thought. Being lost in thought is much better than just being lost, at least I think so. Anyway, I was lost in thought and another water walker (no, it wasn't Jesus; this person was in the water, not on the water) asked, "What are you thinking about?"

I said, "Heaven," and shared my worries about the eternal banquet.

When I said that I did not think Cathy the cow would find being eaten heavenly, my friend said, "Manna. We will eat manna for eternity."

I thought, *That is ludicrous.* The Hebrews were darned tired of eating manna after only forty years. Eating manna for an eternity would be awful. Besides, *manna* means "What is it?" Can you imagine eating "What is it?" for eternity?

Can you imagine a conversation around manna?

Phil, one of my infinite number of friends in heaven, we will have nothing but friends in Heaven so this is really a ridiculous statement. Anyway, Phil asks me, "What are you having for dinner?"

I say, "This."

Phil says, "What is it?"

I say, "Yep."

Pointing to the manna, Phil says, "What is it?"

I say, "Exactly."

His face getting red and his voice is rising, Phil says, "Are you being a smart butt? What are you eating for dinner?"

I say, "What is it?"

Phil, his face contorting, says, "What is what? Dinner? Are you asking what dinner is?"

I say, "No. I know what dinner is."

Phil, visibly upset, just gives me a big huff turns and leaves saying, "I will never talk to you again."

I say, "Are we still friends?"

Phil shouts over his shoulder, "No."

Now everyone in Heaven is no longer friends; all because of Manna. This is why we are not eating manna for eternity.

The whole banquet theory falls apart pretty quickly when you think about it.

I also must confess that I like to sing. But this does not mean that I am any good at it. Nor does it mean that others like to listen to me sing. I have heard more than my share of bad singing, most often; usually in the form of special music when someone comes forward during church services. A sound track is turned on, and suddenly it is karaoke morning in church. I hope that heaven is more than singing—not just for my sake, but for the sake of those standing in earshot of my voice.

When I talk to people about singing in heaven and tell them that I can't sing, they say, "When you get to heaven God will give you a wonderful voice." I cannot help but think, *It will be like those Allstate commercials where the little girl is talking to her dad and suddenly her voice changes into this beautiful baritone and she says, "Allstate—you have the Allstate protection plan."* Her father looks at her in wonderment. I am sure that he is thinking, *Who is this inside my daughter, and why does my daughter sound like a forty-year-old man?*

I do not know if I will be given a beautiful voice; I do not think that having a new voice is the point of heaven.

As a chaplain, I get to listen to lots of people talk about lots of things. I was sitting with a YMCA member the other day. He had tried to commit suicide and had been in the hospital. He had just been released and came to me for help. He needed someone who could help him work through his problems. He needed a psychologist or a psychiatrist. He had no insurance and little money, thus his dilemma. It took me a couple of hours, but I was able to find him the help he needed. He still likes to sit with me and talk.

After he left, I had another conversation.

I had a conversation with God.

The role was reversed. I did most of the talking and He did the listening.

One of the things that I tell the member who comes to me is that life is worth living even though we do not know all the ins and outs, all the ifs, ands, or buts of the future.

As I was talking with God, He said that heaven is much the same way. Heaven is bigger and better than I can ever imagine. I do not know all the ins and outs, all the ifs, ands, or buts of heaven.

Life is worth living.

Heaven is worth looking forward to.

Have a wonderful day.

Blessings,
Roger

Dramastically

Good morning. I pray that the day finds you well.

We have a funny language.

I think our communication would be clearer and more concise if we were sure of what our words mean when we say them. I know that we have had the word police in the past, but as effective as these people were, as passionate as they always seemed to be—after all, they were unpaid volunteers—their efforts went for naught.

I often think that if we had fewer words or had come up with our own language instead of stealing words and phrases from every other language in the world, we would have an easier time of it.

I was having coffee with a friend of mine today. I will call her Lindsey. As she was telling me about her day, a vital part of any counseling session, she said, "The things that we are doing will dramastically impact us in a good way."

I looked at her and said, "Dramastically? Is that a combination of *dramatically* and *fantastically*?"

She looked at me, smiled, and said, "Yes."

So often when we talk with one another we use terms and phrases that others may not understand.

An old saying goes, "Listen with the intent to listen and not with the intent to respond."

Still another old saying advises, "Speak with the intent of being understood and not merely heard."

I am not a fan of the word police. As efficient as our language could be if we cut down on the "new" words, it sure would not be as much fun. I never would have learned the word *dramastically* or had the opportunity to use it in a sentence.

I will remember, though, as I go through my day and talk with people, to speak with the intent of being understood and not merely heard. I will listen with the intent to listen and not with the intent to respond.

If my job is to present the good news to people, I better make sure that I am communicating well.

Blessings,
Roger

Making Room for God;
a Forced Sabbath

Good morning. I pray that the day finds you well.

Last Friday around 10:30 a.m., I was sitting in the YMCA membership office. I had already had a meeting and two counseling appointments and had played basketball with Tony and Scotty. (Playing basketball with them is a daily routine. Tony was a star athlete in high school and was all set to go to college on a basketball scholarship when he got into a bad car accident that changed his life forever. A brain injury left him with short-term memory loss and the emotional state of a seventeen-year-old. Scotty was placed on oxygen when he was born and cannot speak. He has the mind of a four-year-old. Tony is forty-five. Scotty is in his twenties.) I had made my morning rounds and was finishing up with membership. It had been a very good week; I had spoken at summer camp staff training sessions, connected with faith community members, done counseling, and found resources for people with problems that included relational difficulties, domestic violence, unemployment, homelessness, and attempted suicide.

I had been working until almost ten every night.

I was sitting in the office, checking in with the membership staff. A typical check-in goes like this:

Me: "Good morning."
Staff member: "Good morning."
Me: "How are you doing today?"
Staff member: "Okay." (This is an opportunity for me.)
Me: "Just okay? How come you are just okay?"

Staff members will tell me what is bothering them and making their day just okay. I will talk with them about this and try to reframe situations and refocus people's thoughts.

Last Friday, as I offered morning greetings, this is what happened.

A staff member turned toward me and said, "Roger, you look terrible."

I am not one of those guys who spend a lot of time making sure every hair is in place before they go out the door, but I do shower, shave, comb my hair, and try to look decent, so being told I looked "terrible" set me back a bit. I hoped that I would get an explanation, and I did.

A board member was walking by and stopped in to say hello. This person said, "Roger, you look terrible," pointing out the bags under my eyes and noting my exhausted appearance.

I thought, *Thanks a lot.*

Then something amazing happened.

One of the staff asked to see my phone. I gave it to her.

She then called the people with whom I had scheduled appointments for the weekend and explained that I was exhausted and couldn't make it. She said that the staff was worried about my health and that I was to do nothing but rest over the weekend. She then e-mailed my wife to say that I was looking very tired and should take time off.

I was shocked. I was amazed.

Both the board member and the staff member told me, "Roger, you spend your entire day looking after us. You take on the troubles of the staff, the members, and the community. We are only looking after you."

I admitted that I was feeling a little run-down.

Sometimes God shows up in the funniest places.

Sometimes we see Him in the blue sky and the clouds.

Sometimes we see Him when we walk in the country.

Sometimes we see Him in a staff member and a board member.

I went home. My wife met me at the door and made me take a nap.

It is Sunday morning. I have rested and am feeling much better. I will spend the rest of the day puttering in my yard and thanking God for the people who care enough to tell me when to go home.

One of the dangers of living your calling is that it does not feel like work.

I counsel people and tell everyone I talk with about the importance of taking a sabbath.

I am terrible at taking a sabbath. I must learn to follow what I ask others to do.

Thank You, God, for showing up through a couple of people at the YMCA.

Blessings,
Roger

A Quiet Morning

Good morning. I pray that the day finds you well.

The seasons are changing. Actually that is a silly phrase; the seasons are always changing. I am reminded of what a weatherman once said. (I guess if I were being politically correct, I would say *weatherperson*, but this was a guy, so I think I am safe saying *weatherman*. Maybe not. I don't know.) He told viewers, "There was no weather today." I thought, *What a silly thing to say. Of course there was weather today. There is always weather.*

It is getting a bit cooler, and the mornings are dark when I wake up at my house by the river. The birds are still asleep and the air is still. We have an interesting phenomenon where I live. The sun heats the air and causes it to move through the valleys and along the rivers, creating a gentle breeze. Because there was no sun this morning, there was no breeze.

I sat in my chair, listening to the river.

I sat in my chair, waiting to hear the first rustlings of the birds and the other animals that call the river home.

I sat in my chair, waiting to hear the waking of the day.

I sat in my chair, listening for God.

God did not say anything.

After a while, I got up from my chair and prepared to go to the Y.

I got dressed and collected the things that I needed for the day. When I got in the car, I realized I had forgotten my keys. I went back to the house, got my keys, got back into the car, and started driving to work.

As I drove into town, I noticed noise. I was stopped at a stoplight (which is a lot better than driving through a stoplight), when I noticed the music coming from a car that pulled up next to me. I noticed the engine noise from a nearby truck. Pretty soon I was noticing a lot of noises.

Then a still small voice said, "The world is full of noise. I gave you this morning so that you could remember the tranquility and draw on that in the midst of the noise of the day."

As I went through my day and listened to noise, I was thankful that God caused me to stop and realize that I can draw on the quiet times. If I am to be an ambassador of Christ, I must not allow myself to be caught up in the noise of the day, but be a respite for people who have fallen into this trap.

Lord, I pray that You continue to give me grace as I do my best to abide in You as you are abiding in me. Let me be that quiet moment for people when they can sit and decompress, when they can sit and be in You as You are in them. Amen.

Blessings,
Roger

Getting on Right Race Boulevard

Good morning. I pray that the day finds you well.

I hit the ground running this morning.

I did not get much sleep last night. It was one of those nights when I kept waking up—so many thoughts, so little time.

When I got to the Y, I faced a barrage of e-mails, phone calls, and individual needs.

I was multitasking. I was responding to e-mails while answering phone calls.

Brandon, the pastor of the church that meets at our Y, and I would be on the phone when an emergency call would come through, and I would have to hang up on him and take the call. Fortunately, Brandon and I have a good working relationship and he knows my heart.

Then the noise began. Right outside my wall, the impact hammers started up. I could not hear anything else, and I knew I had to grab my cell phone and my iPad and find a quiet place that had wireless so I could continue my day.

I was walking to my car with my cell phone, iPad, keys, and coffee cup (a vital part of my ministry) when my phone rang. I answered and asked if I could have a moment to get into my car. The caller said says yes. I entered my car, threw my iPad, phone, and keys on the passenger seat, put my coffee cup to my ear, and said, "I am back." I realized that I was talking into the cup. I put it down, picked up my iPhone, and hit the end button, cutting myself off. I called the person back, and he asked, "What happened?" I told him I was busy talking to my coffee cup and hung up on him when I realized I was not on the phone.

This is when I knew beyond a doubt that I had completely fallen into the rat race.

I am now in a quiet space where I can take a moment to breathe and wait on the Lord.

The rat race is insidious. You can be in it before you know it and without even trying. Even if you are intentional about avoiding this trap, it will sneak up on you.

The goal is not to go into hiding to escape the race. It would be very hard, even impossible, to be in active ministry living as a hermit, so being a hermit is not the goal. The goal is to have your rat race radar on so that you realize quickly what is happening and can make adjustments to get off of Rat Race Highway and onto Right Race Boulevard.

Father, continue to give me nudges so that I can exit Rat Race Highway and enter Right Race Boulevard. Guide me. Be my GPS if You will, and continue to teach me so that I can present my best self to others so that they may know You. Amen.

Blessings,
Roger

Roses or Fish Bombs?

Good morning. I pray that the day finds you well.

Memory is a funny thing. I will go a long time without thinking of something or someone, but when I do, it is as if my memory is doing a data dump on my consciousness.

I hadn't thought about Fishmonger for years, but ever since the other night she has been on my brain.

Fish lived to be almost twenty years old, and so she was around from the time I was six until after I had left the house for good. Anyone with children in college would understand this situation. I boomeranged for a while. Just when my parents thought I was grown and out of the house, I would come running through the front door, usually with an armload of laundry. Sometimes I would tie a ribbon around it and try to pass it off as a gift for my mom.

It never worked.

All this is to say that Fish grew up and grew old.

As Fish aged, her hobbies changed. Where once she could not get enough of mousing, she didn't seem as excited about this pursuit later in life. On one of my boomerang trips, I sat with Fish on the floor in the basement of my parents' house, watching *Nightline with Ted Koppel*. As we listened to Ted offer his journalistic wisdom, a mouse ran by right in front of us. Actually, its pace was more like a jog (if mice can jog).

Fish didn't move.

I thought she must be asleep. I looked down at her, and she looked up at me as if to say, "What? I'm retired." It was left to me to get up, catch the mouse, and put it back outside. I am sure the mouse soon returned from where it had been deposited.

But Fish found new hobbies.

Her new favorite hobby was to visit people as they entered the house and sat in the living room. She would say hello, then leave the room only to sneak back behind the couch and leave what became known affectionately as a "Fish bomb." These rancid, slow-moving odors always seemed to stall out in the middle of the room. Usually the only relief that one could find was to go outside until the smell dissipated or Mom retaliated with often-copious amounts of Lysol.

I grew up with three sisters. With a sister comes the inevitable boyfriend, who has the annoying habit of hanging out at his girlfriend's house.

As you might guess, my sisters' boyfriends always had a "first time" at their girlfriends' house.

The first time was always the same.

Fish would come into the living room and say hello.

Fish would leave the room.

Fish would then sneak back into the room behind the couch.

Fish would leave a bomb.

Fish would then leave the room.

People would look at each other, knowing that they did not do it.

People would leave the house, and Mom would arrive to battle the bomb.

You are probably wondering where all this is going.

As I recalled Fish and the bomb, I thought about how we sometimes leave a wake of pain behind us when we are focused on ourselves and not on others.

When we focus on others and put their needs above our own, we leave roses and smiles.

The question is, when we leave the room, do we want others to smell roses or Fish bombs?

Something to think about.

Blessings,
Roger

May the peace of the Lord Christ go with you,
Wherever He may send you.
May He guide you through the wilderness,
Protect you through the storm.
May he bring you home rejoicing
At the wonders He has shown you.
May He bring you home rejoicing
Once again into our doors.[7]

Go in peace.

---

[7] Northumbria Community, *Celtic Daily Prayer,* (San Francisco: HarperCollins Publishing Company, 2002), 19.

Bibliography

Bible. *New International Version.* Grand Rapids: Zondervan. 1984.

Bonhoeffer, Dietrich. *I Want to Live These Days with You: A Year of Daily Devotions.* Louisville: Westminster John Knox Press, 2005.

Chambers, Oswald. *My Utmost for His Highest.* Uhrichsville: Barbour Publishing, 1935.

http://www.merriam-webster.com/dictionary/simplex viewed June 6, 2012.

Northumbria Community. *Celtic Daily Prayer.* San Francisco: HarperCollins Publishing Company, 2002.

Sweet, Leonard Sweet., *Viral.* Colorado Springs: WaterBrook Press, 2012.

39047852R00099

Made in the USA
Middletown, DE
03 January 2017